Bright Start

Activities to Develop Your Child's Potential

Writer:
Michael K. Meyerhoff, Ed.D.

PUBLICATIONS INTERNATIONAL, LTD.

Michael K. Meyerhoff, Ed.D., is the executive director of The Epicenter, Inc., an agency that monitors academic, commercial, and popular activities in early childhood and parent education. He serves as adjunct professor of early childhood at the National College of Education. Dr. Meyerhoff is the coauthor of *The Complete Book of Parenting*, and his articles have appeared in numerous publications for parents, including *American Baby*, *Young Children*, and *Parent & Preschooler*. He received his bachelor's degree in psychology from Columbia University and earned his master's degree and doctorate in human development from the Harvard Graduate School of Education.

Illustrations: George Ulrich, Terri and Joe Chicko

Manufactured in China.

8 7 6 5 4 3 2 1

ISBN: 0-7853-4902-2

Library of Congress Control Number: 2001116324

Contents

Introduction

Is playing with very young children enough? In today's competitive, ever-changing world, many parents wonder if they should be doing something more. After all, recent research clearly indicates that success in school—and in life—depends heavily on an abundance of appropriate educational experiences during the critical early years. Like most parents, you want to give your children every possible advantage right from the start. The question is, how?

Fortunately, research also indicates that for infants, babies, toddlers, and preschoolers, "having fun" and "learning" are one and the same. It is through productive and pleasurable play activities that young children build wide and firm foundations for later academic achievement. These activities help them develop the broad concepts and general skills they will use to master challenges in the years to come.

Bright Start is filled with a great variety of activities that incorporate this special combination of enjoyment and education. As you peruse and pursue each one, always keep in mind the following basic principles derived from the most reliable and reputable research on learning during the early years:

I. *"Learning to learn" is the most important lesson of the early years.*

Children are born with an incredible amount of curiosity. However, before they can learn all they want and need to learn, they first must learn how to learn. They must figure out how to absorb information from the environment, how to adapt their knowledge and skills to different situations, and how to solve whatever problems arise. Since every child has a unique style of learning, this cannot be achieved through instruction. But through fun and stimulating activities, such as those in *Bright Start*, children can discover for themselves which strategies are most comfortable and effective.

The lessons of the early years should address the "whole child." Young children are interested in learning about everything all the time. They don't benefit, as older students do, from having specific subjects presented to them according to a structured agenda. The whole world is brand new and tremendously exciting to small children, and they will use all their interactions with people and objects to make connections and to further every aspect of their development—physical, intellectual, linguistic, social, and emotional.

To better understand how each activity fosters your child's development, read the brief explanation in the "Building Blocks" section of each page. But keep in mind that each activity in *Bright Start* has multiple purposes—not the least of which is having a good time with your child. These play activities give children a smorgasbord of learning opportunities from which they can choose the particular experiences that are most helpful and meaningful to them at the moment.

2. *Early educational development proceeds horizontally as well as vertically.*

Educational development is not like climbing a ladder, where reaching one rung is a signal to move immediately up to the next. Instead, it's more like constructing a pyramid, where the higher levels must be fully supported by the lower ones. Therefore, during the early years, children need to spend time making the foundations for later academic achievement as broad and solid as possible. They do this by extensive repetition of favorite activities along with gradual expansion and elaboration through activities with similar themes. Repetition does not waste precious time. Rather, it helps children make substantial progress in building a strong and stable educational structure.

3. *Every child exhibits a unique rate and pattern of educational progress during the early years.*

Like sunsets, snowflakes, and other miracles of nature, no two children are exactly alike. And learning is a process, not a race. So, when it comes to educational development during the early years, it is critical to keep in mind that "different" does not automatically imply "better" or "worse" and that "equal" does not necessarily mean "identical."

The *Bright Start* activities have been grouped into chapters according to the chronological age periods in which they probably will be most appropriate. But some children may enjoy an activity or two a little earlier, and some may not be inclined to pursue an activity or two until a little later. Remember that the easiest and most effective way to educate children is to let them learn what they want when they want to learn it. Pushing children into an activity for which they are not quite ready will ultimately be counterproductive. As long as their individual rate and pattern of progress is respected, learning will be fun and self-sustaining. These activities should always be exciting challenges leading to personal fulfillment and should never become chores to be completed merely to obtain adult approval.

4. *Educational activities are greatly enhanced by enthusiastic and conscientious parental involvement.*

You are your child's first and most important teacher. You also are her favorite playmate. Consequently, the *Bright Start* activities have been designed to ensure that through your active involvement, your child will receive the maximum amount of education and enjoyment. Furthermore, these activities are designed to give you ample opportunities to observe and assess your child's constantly expanding interests and steadily increasing abilities. While professional educators can be considered experts on young children in general, no one is better qualified to be an expert on your child than you.

Think of *Bright Start* as a valuable resource for promoting your child's educational development, not as a rigid "recipe" that must be followed precisely. You have a unique ability to identify your child's current interests and abilities and to select, vary, and guide the activities accordingly.

As the weeks, months, and years go by, children make incredible strides in preparations for academic success. Eventually, they will start to benefit from more direct instruction on specific subjects in a formal setting. However, during the early years, it is reassuring to know that the most accurate way to monitor children's educational progress is simply to notice how much fun they are having.

Chapter 1
Birth to 3 Months

Infants sleep a lot during their first three months of life. It takes time to adjust to the differences between the womb and the outside world, so infants don't have much desire to interact with their surroundings. Attempts to stimulate newborns during the first few weeks of life are futile, and babies may find them intrusive and irritating.

But when they're awake and alert, newborns use their senses to absorb as much information as possible from their environment. Gradually, infants will start to exercise their bodies and discover the vari-

ous movements they can make. By the end of this period, infants begin to control and even to coordinate body movements, using them in conjunction with their senses. The first smiles appear at about two months of age, and infants become increasingly sociable.

Sock It to Me

Infants find their feet by wearing these colorful and musical socks.

What You'll Need:

several pairs of infant socks

needle and thread

plastic rings

jingle bells

yarn pom-pom

fabric paint or fabric markers

Sew rings or bells on a pair of infant socks or booties, and sew pom-poms on others. Make sure they are attached securely and can't be pulled off. Draw colorful pictures and patterns on the socks. When the infant is awake and alert, slip a pair on her feet for a few minutes. (Be sure to closely supervise.) Use different pairs of socks on different days. The infant will be treated to a variety of auditory and visual experiences whenever she wiggles and kicks her feet. As the weeks go by, she will gradually gain more control over her legs and be able to bring her feet closer to her face. Eventually, she also will learn to move in ways that cause her favorite sounds to be repeated and her favorite sights to reappear.

Building Blocks

This activity helps infants begin to understand the consequences of their movements.

Nifty Necklaces

Wear these necklaces to improve your infant's visual skills and refine his reaching ability.

What You'll Need:

strong cord or yarn

large beads

plastic rings

String the cord or yarn through a variety of bright and boldly colored beads and rings. Tie large knots between the items to keep them separated. Tie the ends together to make a necklace using a strong knot that will not come undone easily. The cord should be long enough so that the beads and rings are within the infant's reach when you bend over him, but not so long that the items bang into his face. When you're diapering, dressing, or bathing the infant, he will be dazzled by the colorful objects dangling above him. As the weeks go by, he will begin reaching for the interesting objects and use his new-found eye-hand coordination to grab for them with steadily increasing accuracy.

Building Blocks

This activity encourages infants to discover and practice visually directed reaching.

Visual Tracker

Focus-Pocus! Help your baby improve her ability to follow moving objects with her eyes.

What You'll Need:

small assortment of brightly colored objects, such as:

key ring

plastic lid

stuffed animal

ball

When the infant is awake and alert and lying on her back, lean over her so your face is approximately 8 inches from her eyes. Slowly move your face from side to side, making sure that it is never more than 12 inches away. At first, she will attempt to track your moving face with jerky movements of her head and eyes. But with time and practice, she soon will be tracking smoothly. As her tracking ability improves, hold various objects over her and repeat the exercise. When she's almost three months old, help her practice focusing, too. Slowly move your face and the objects closer to her face and then farther away. Watch her carefully as you do so. If you lose her attention too quickly, you may be stretching her still-imperfect visual skills too far.

Building Blocks

This activity helps infants learn to control their vision and to collect sensory information more effectively.

For the first few days, infants will be alert only about three minutes per hour. However, periods of alertness steadily increase over the next few weeks, more than doubling in length after just one month.

Magic Carpet Ride

Give your infant a scenic ride through friendly territory.

What You'll Need:

**soft, thick blanket
or towel**

Building Blocks

This activity gives pre-mobile infants the opportunity to move through their environment, having different visual and auditory experiences.

Place a soft, thick blanket or towel on the floor of any room that has a smooth surface (tile, linoleum, or hardwood). Place the infant on his back in the middle of the blanket or towel. Bend down, grab the end, and then slowly and gently pull it around the room. During the tour, keep up a running commentary, describing all the new and different sights he sees. At first, be sure to talk about the objects and scenes that are right next to him. Later, as his focusing ability improves, describe things that are increasingly farther away. As soon as the infant shows signs of being able to roll over, discontinue this activity, as he may accidentally fall off during the ride.

Batter Up

You pitch, she swings! Help your infant improve her body control and refine visually directed reaching skills.

What You'll Need:

scissors

sturdy cord

large beads or plastic rings

short pole or dowel rod

Cut the cord into short pieces. Loop each piece through a bead or ring. Secure the ends to the pole or rod with a strong knot. When the infant is awake and alert, hold the pole or rod over the crib or changing table so that the objects are within a comfortable arm's reach. Allow her to reach for, swipe at, and bat the suspended objects. To avoid frustration, make sure the objects do not sway too much when hit and that they quickly return to their original positions. Since the infant is just learning to use her hands under the direction of her eyes, she may initially need several attempts before she is able to make contact. Targets that move far away or fast are too challenging at this early point in development.

Building Blocks

This activity helps infants coordinate their improving sensory skills with their emerging motor abilities.

Touchy Subjects

This touchy-feely activity increases body awareness, stimulates tactile skills, and promotes language development.

What You'll Need:

large assortment of fabric scraps (such as silk, corduroy, satin, velvet, and wool)

When the infant is awake and alert, take different pieces of fabric and gently rub them along different parts of his body. As you do so, describe the texture and label the part of his body you're touching. For example, say, "This feels rough on your arm, this feels smooth on your tummy" or "this feels soft on your face." Watch the infant's face closely for his reactions. Repeat the sensations he likes and discontinue any that make him uncomfortable. This activity can be varied and expanded by including different articles of clothing (leather glove, felt hat, feather boa) and suitable household objects (marble dish, stuffed animal, metal spoon). When appropriate, mention the temperature of the objects ("warm" and "cool"). Never use items that are hot or cold to the touch.

Building Blocks

This activity nurtures the roots of sensory discrimination and lays the groundwork for connections between words and the objects and sensations they represent.

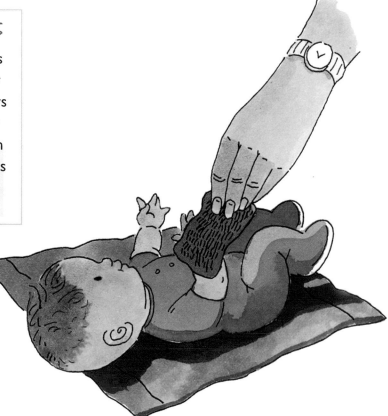

Focusing on Faces

Sit-ups with your infant are good for you and for her, too!

Lie on your back on a soft, flat, comfortable surface. Prop the infant so that her back rests comfortably against your legs. Keep your hands on her body at all times, holding her gently but securely in place. Slowly do "sit-ups," gradually bringing your face into her focus, holding it there for a few seconds, and then gradually lowering it back down. As you move, describe to the infant what is happening ("I'm coming to you, here I am, I'm going away"). You can make this activity more entertaining by making a different face each time you reappear (smiling, frowning, acting surprised) and adding appropriate comments and exclamations ("Hello, how are you, good-bye").

Building Blocks

This activity encourages infants to practice visual skills as their favorite "target" moves in and out of range.

Lots of exposure to human speech greatly enhances early language development. But only real human voices are effective. Input from a television, radio, or other electronic device does not make a significant difference.

Audio Feedback

Tape record and play back your infant's vocalizations.

What You'll Need:

tape cassette player

blank tape

Use the cassette player and tape to record the sounds your baby makes. Keep it handy so it is available during feeding, bathing, diapering, and other activities when he is likely to cry, gurgle, coo, and otherwise express himself. Then, at a time when he is awake and alert but quiet, play the tape back for him. Describe what he is hearing ("That's you crying because you had a wet diaper; That's you telling me you liked the way you were being rocked"). Watch his reaction to the sounds carefully. Play the ones he seems to prefer over and over again, and avoid those that appear to cause him any kind of distress. Make a new recording every week or so to capture the new sounds he's making.

Good Vibrations

From the TV to the washing machine, it's time to rumble.

What You'll Need:

soft blanket

well-designed infant seat

Building Blocks

This activity helps infants learn to absorb information from a variety of sources using all of their sensory mechanisms.

Place the infant on your chest. Make deep rumbling sounds and let her feel the vibrations on different parts of her body. Place your lips on different parts of her body and hum. Place her on a blanket on top of a television console when the set is turned on. Hold her securely and let her feel those vibrations. Secure the infant in an infant seat and place it on top of the washing machine during the agitation and spin cycles, letting her feel other kinds of vibrations. Take careful note of her reactions. Quickly remove her if anything seems to cause distress, and allow her to linger with anything she seems to find particularly entertaining. If something appears to be especially soothing, keep it in mind for times when the infant may be having trouble being comforted or falling asleep.

Head-Lift Fun

Help your infant practice and improve his large muscle skills.

What You'll Need:

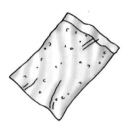

soft blanket

Lay the blanket on a flat, comfortable surface. Place the infant on the blanket, tummy down. Lie down facing him, so that your face is within his focus. When you have his attention, slowly raise your head, saying "Up, up, up!" as he attempts to lift his head and follow your face, and then "Down, down, down!" as he relaxes his neck muscles. Pay attention to his reaction and be careful not to move too far or too fast. At first, the infant will be able to lift his head only an inch or so for just a second or two. But as the weeks go by, his neck muscles will get stronger and he will be able to lift his head higher and hold it up for longer periods of time.

Building Blocks

This activity helps infants gain control over their head and neck, enabling them to visually explore the environment more effectively.

During the early years, motor development proceeds from head to tail. Body control starts with the head and neck and then gradually moves lower and lower.

At-Home Tourist

Show your infant a whole new world at home.

What You'll Need:

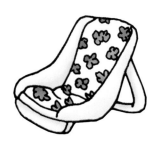

**well-designed
infant seat**

By the end of the third month, infants are able to see and hear everything going on about them quite clearly—and they are increasingly curious about it all. Unfortunately, they still will not have the ability to move on their own. At regular intervals throughout the day, place your infant in the infant seat and secure her comfortably. Then move her about the house and give her different scenes to look at and listen to. Place her in the kitchen while dinner is being made. Place her in the laundry room when the wash is being done. Place her next to a window when the wind is blowing or traffic is going by. Take note of the activities and events she seems to find particularly fascinating, and talk to her about what is happening and what you are doing.

Building Blocks

This activity increases the infant's range of experiences while also expanding her exposure to and awareness of language.

By the end of the third month, infants are able to accurately and reliably distinguish the faces and voices of their parents from those of other people.

Family Line-Up

Get the whole family involved in helping your infant practice visual and auditory discrimination.

What You'll Need:

well-designed infant seat, or bed and pillows, or sofa and cushions

Using a well-designed infant seat, a bed and pillows, or a sofa and cushions, prop the infant in a comfortable and secure semi-reclining position. By bending or kneeling down, slowly move your face into his field of vision, hold it there for a minute, then slowly move it away. Keep in mind that until he is a few weeks old, he will be able to focus clearly only if your face is between 8 and 12 inches from his eyes. While you are in front of the infant, identify yourself and tell him something ("This is Mommy, and I love you very much"). Have other family members repeat the exercise in turn ("I'm Daddy, and I think you're cute" and "My name is Timmy, and I'm your big brother"). Avoid confusing the infant by limiting the "introductions" to those people with whom he interacts on a regular basis.

Building Blocks

This activity encourages infants to attend to differences in sensory input and to make connections between visual and auditory cues.

Chapter 2
3 to 6 Months

Between three and six months of age, infants gain much more control over their bodies. Their focus improves, and they regularly use their hands under the guidance of their eyes. They eagerly reach for and grab anything they can, bringing it closer to explore and investigate with their hands, fingers, and mouth. Infants at this age also become increasingly interested in the effects of their actions. They are fascinated by language and start to experiment with their own vocalizations. And now that they have a strong sense of self, they delight in any and all interactions with their favorite people.

Beginning Anatomy

You're the instructor for these basic body and language lessons.

While you're bathing, diapering, or dressing your infant, gently touch, rub, and squeeze different parts of his body. Say "hand," "ear," "tummy," "leg," or whatever is appropriate as you focus his attention on a particular part. Start with just three or four parts, and repeat them several times. Gradually add other body parts to lessons later on. Pay careful attention to what the infant is doing. If he moves a particular part on his own, make sure to touch and label it for him right away. After a while, introduce action words along with the corresponding motions. For example, hold his hands and lightly clap them together saying, "We are clapping hands!" Or hold his feet and move his legs in a circular bicycling pattern saying, "We are getting ready to ride a tricycle!"

During the early years, motor development proceeds in a near to far direction. That is, body control starts with the torso, then gradually moves to the arms and legs, then to the hands, and finally to the fingers.

Building Blocks

This activity encourages infants to develop connections between their sensory or motor experiences and the words that identify or describe them.

Sight and Sound Machines

Shake, rattle, and roll! These homemade toys help your infant learn about cause and effect.

What You'll Need:

small plastic screw-cap bottles

multicolored collections of buttons, beads, and dry cereals

glue

Fill some bottles with buttons, some with beads, some with cereal, and some with various combinations of these materials. Leave a little room in each bottle so the materials can move about and make noise when they're shaken. Glue the caps on the bottles securely. When the glue is dry, pick up the bottles and shake them in front of the infant. Then place the bottles all around her so they are within her reach. Let her grab them and shake them, too. Roll the bottles back and forth on the floor in front of the infant. If she shows interest in rolling the bottles herself, let her push them along the floor. But be prepared to retrieve and replace any bottles that travel out of her reach.

Building Blocks

This activity lets infants practice hand-eye coordination and increases their awareness of the connection between their actions and the consequences of them.

Send Back the Sound

Imitate your infant, and he won't just be flattered.
He'll become familiar with language patterns.

Sit in front of your infant when he is fully awake and alert. Whenever he makes a sound, such as a gurgle, coo, or babble, react with exaggerated delight. Smile broadly, lift your eyebrows, wave and clap your hands. Then repeat the sound back to him. Watch for the infant's reaction. If he expresses delight as well, or if he makes the sound again, keep repeating the exercise. If the infant's response is relatively passive, introduce new sounds yourself. Start with simple vocalizations such as "ooohs" and "aaahs." Then try more complicated sounds such as tongue-clucking and "blowing raspberries." If the infant reacts with delight to any of the sounds, make sure to repeat them several times, even if he is unable or unwilling to mimic them.

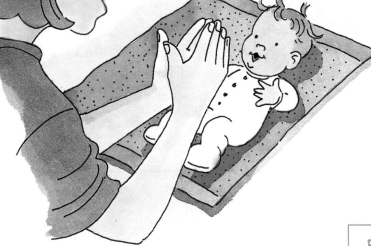

During the first months of life, infants will cry only as a reflexive reaction to physical discomfort of some kind. But by 5 or 6 months of age, they also will intentionally cry in response to boredom.

Building Blocks

This activity promotes the development of linguistic abilities and interpersonal communication skills.

Musical Motion

Got rhythm? Help your infant learn the relationship between movement and music.

What You'll Need:

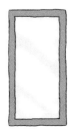

full-length mirror

CD or tape player

collection of favorite tunes

Sit in front of the mirror and place your infant comfortably and securely on your lap. Play a variety of different tunes, holding the infant gently as you move to the music. Describe both the rate and pattern of the motions you are making ("We are swaying back and forth, very slowly; we are bouncing up and down, faster and faster; we are rocking back and forth, leaning backward and forward; we are clapping softly"). If the piece you are listening to is instrumental, make up suitable lyrics and sing your descriptions. Notice which music and movements the infant finds particularly entertaining, and make sure to repeat those several times. Also notice the music and movements she finds especially soothing; they can be effective when she has trouble falling asleep or being comforted.

Building Blocks

This activity promotes auditory discrimination and encourages infants to exercise control over their bodies.

Multitude of Tickles

A tickle here and a tickle there helps your infant learn about his body and increases his sensory-discrimination skills.

What You'll Need:

feather

hat tassel

blanket fringe

cotton ball

satin ribbon

Use your fingers to lightly and gently tickle the infant on different parts of his body. Avoid any areas where tickling seems to cause discomfort, and concentrate on those where it appears to bring him delight. Talk to him about what you are doing and where you are doing it ("I'm tickling your tummy!"). Use each of the different items in turn to give him a variety of tickling experiences, and describe what's happening ("The feather is tickling your foot!"). Start with large areas of the infant's body, such as his hands, feet, arms, legs, and tummy. Gradually move to smaller parts, such as his ears, nose, fingers, and toes. If the infant grabs any of the items, allow him to use his hands, fingers, and mouth to explore their different textures for a few minutes (but make sure he does not eat them).

Building Blocks

This activity expands the infant's tactile experiences and encourages him to make connections between words and the sensations or activities they represent.

Squat Thrusts

Infants love to practice standing on your tummy!

Lie down on your back on a flat, comfortable surface. Place the baby in a standing position on your tummy. Gently hold her hands to keep her steady. Allow the infant to squat and then thrust her legs to bring herself back to a standing position. Describe what the infant is doing by saying, "Down you go, now you're going up!" Whenever the infant has completed a full down-and-up cycle, give her a big cheer and clap her hands together. If the infant bends only one leg or bends each leg alternately, react to that enthusiastically as well. Describe those movements, too, saying, "You're hopping!" or "You're getting ready to run!" or "Look at you dance!" If the infant lowers herself to a sitting position, describe and applaud that, too, noting whether she is getting tired.

The enthusiastic reactions of parents to early physical accomplishments becomes internalized by the infant and forms the foundation for self-esteem and healthy pride in achievement.

Building Blocks
This activity helps improve gross motor abilities and prepares infants for crawling and walking.

Dancing Shadows

It's a bird, it's a plane, it's . . . your shadow!

What You'll Need:

**small lamp or
large flashlight**

Close all drapes or blinds so the room is as dark as possible. Place a lamp or flashlight on a table or shelf, behind where you will be sitting. Sit a few feet away from the blank wall, holding the infant comfortably and securely on your lap. Turn on the lamp or flashlight. Use your arm, hand, and fingers to make various shadows appear on the wall. Describe to the infant the images that appear ("That looks like a bird flying away!"). Hold the infant's arms and use them to make shadows, too. Give the infant opportunities to move and make shadows on his own. Make sure to provide plenty of praise as you describe the results of his efforts ("Those are pretty waves you're making!").

Building Blocks

This activity exposes infants to special aspects of their environment and allows them to investigate some novel consequences of their movements.

Listen and Locate

Can your infant find you using her eyes and ears?

When the infant is awake and alert, stand in front of her and softly call her name. If she looks up at you and smiles, go to a different position in the room and repeat the exercise. Stand off to each side and behind her, and softly call her name again. Give the infant a chance to locate you with her eyes after she has heard your voice. It is a good idea to play this game on a regular basis, starting when the infant is about four months of age. If she repeatedly shows no interest or appears to have difficulty picking up your voice, it might indicate a mild hearing loss. Make sure she is examined by a pediatrician so that any problem, such as an ear infection, can be diagnosed and treated before it has a chance to interfere with language development.

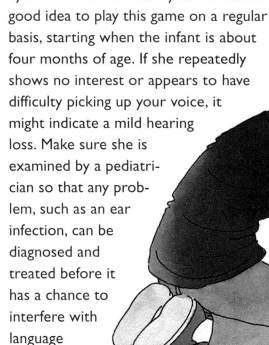

Building Blocks

This activity lets infants practice using both their eyes and ears and ensures that language development can proceed properly.

Extensive research has revealed there is no such thing as the "Mozart Effect." While babies clearly enjoy and probably benefit from exposure to music, there is no evidence to suggest that any particular selections have a special power to promote any specific abilities.

Stretch and Snatch

Help your infant develop hand-eye coordination.

What You'll Need:

favorite toy

Building Blocks

This activity allows infants to investigate and improve their visually directed reaching skills.

Take one of the infant's favorite toys and hold it directly in front of him. After he has grabbed it and played with it for a while, take it from him and hold it a little farther away. Repeat the exercise several times with gradually increasing distance, but make sure to keep the toy within arm's length to avoid frustration. Once the infant is comfortable with the routine, hold the toy at varying distances off to each side. Finally, try introducing motion. Move the toy slowly from side to side or back and forth as he attempts to grab it. Do not play "keep away." Allow the infant to grab the toy quickly, but encourage him to follow the toy with his eyes and alter the direction of his reach a little before he grabs it.

Reverse Piggies

Your fingers are the pig that the baby grabs in this fun game.

This little piggy...

Sit in front of the infant. Present her with each of your fingers in turn. As she grasps each one, say, "This little piggy went to market, this little piggy stayed home, this little piggy had roast beef, this little piggy had none, and this little piggy cried wee-wee-wee all the way home!" Add an exaggerated "Oooh!" or "Ahhh!" whenever she succeeds in grasping your finger. If the infant enjoys the game, increase the challenge by moving each finger slightly from side to side or forward and back when you present it to her. Feel free to make up your own commentary for the game or variations on the standard rhyme. Just make sure to keep the commentary consistent so the infant will have little trouble taking over the announcing role later on when her language skills develop.

It is impossible to tickle an infant prior to 3 months of age because tickling is an interpersonal as well as a physical activity. It is not until 3 months of age that the infant has enough social awareness to fully appreciate the fact that he is the "ticklee" and someone else is the "tickler."

Building Blocks

This activity helps refine small muscle and visual skills and promotes language awareness.

Natural Textures

Nature provides many different textures for your infant to feel.

What You'll Need:

cardboard

glue

variety of natural objects, such as leaves, rocks, twigs, and flower petals

Building Blocks

This activity helps infants refine their sensory discrimination skills and exposes them to novel words and phrases.

Glue each of the items to the cardboard. Make sure all edges of the leaves and flower petals are securely fastened to the cardboard so the infant can't pick them apart and eat them. Place the cardboard in front of the infant and gently guide his hands to each item. Encourage him to touch and rub them. As he does so, describe what each item is and what it feels like ("That's a rock, it's gray, hard, and rough; that's a leaf, it's green, smooth, and slippery"). Dispose of the board when the biodegradable items begin to decompose. Make new boards, adding new and different items each time. In addition or as an option, make other boards using common household items with different textures.

Beach Ball Balance

Rolling on a beach ball gives your infant new sensory and motor experiences.

What You'll Need:

large inflatable beach ball

Fully inflate the beach ball and place it on the floor. Place the infant tummy down on top of the beach ball. Hold her gently but securely and slowly roll the ball from side to side and back and forth. Describe the motions, saying, "You are rolling to the left, you are rolling to the right, you are rolling forward, you are rolling backward." Note the infant's reactions. If she's delighted by the motions, gradually increase the speed and length of the rolls within safe limits. If she seems distressed, reduce the speed and length of the rolls and then gradually increase them as she becomes more comfortable. In addition or as an option, lay the infant on the floor and roll the ball from side to side and back and forth across her body, but be sure to avoid her face.

Building Blocks

This activity helps infants develop a sense of balance.

Elevator Operator

Going up and coming down helps your infant develop his focus.

Lie down on your back on a flat, comfortable surface. Hold the infant over you, tummy down, and give him a chance to focus on your face. Then slowly and gently push him up, saying, "Up, up, up, higher, higher, higher!" When your arms are fully outstretched, hold the infant in that position for a few seconds. Then slowly and gently lower him down, saying, "Down, down, down, lower, lower, lower." When the infant's face reaches yours, give him a big kiss and hold him stationary for a few seconds. Then repeat the exercise. During subsequent sessions, introduce variations in speed and pattern, adding side to side and circular motions. Make sure to describe these additions, saying, "Up fast, down slow!" or "Around and around and around we go!" Always be prepared to reduce the speed or range of motion if the infant shows any signs of distress.

Although children may not fully understand words until the second half of the first year and may not say any words until after the first birthday, research indicates that talking to children as much as possible during the first months of life greatly enhances language development.

Building Blocks

This activity improves the infant's focusing ability and increases his awareness of the connections between words and actions.

Chapter 3

6 to 12 Months

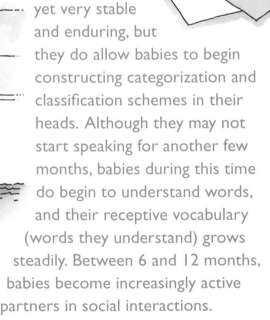

Babies take a giant developmental leap during their second six months of life when they learn to move around by themselves. Their curiosity drives them to explore, investigating every area and object with which they come in contact. For the first time, they are able to make mental images of the information they receive through their senses. These mental images are not yet very stable and enduring, but they do allow babies to begin constructing categorization and classification schemes in their heads. Although they may not start speaking for another few months, babies during this time do begin to understand words, and their receptive vocabulary (words they understand) grows steadily. Between 6 and 12 months, babies become increasingly active partners in social interactions.

Routine Operas

Break out in song to make mundane tasks fun.

Whenever you are dressing, feeding, diapering, or performing any other routine task with the baby, create a "song" that describes the basics of what you are doing. Use an original tune or simply make up new words to a favorite song. For example, instead of the standard lyrics for "I've Been Working on the Railroad," you can sing, "I am taking off your diaper, now I'm throwing it away, I'll be putting on a new one, and then we'll go and play!" Or instead of the standard lyrics to "Old MacDonald Had a Farm," you can sing, "Now your Daddy takes a sponge, E-I-E-I-O, and on that sponge he puts some soap, E-I-E-I-O, with a wipe, wipe here and a wipe, wipe there." Watch the baby's reaction. If she's delighted by the tune, repeat it whenever you perform that particular routine.

Building Blocks

This activity enhances language development and stimulates the development of attention and memory skills.

Babies normally begin to understand language between 6 and 8 months of age. But the normal range that they begin to talk is 6 to 24 months of age. Some babies who are developing superb language skills may not start speaking until they are almost two years old—at which time they may begin speaking in complete sentences.

Floating Fish

How many fishes are swimming in your tub?

What You'll Need:

bathtub or shallow basin

large assortment of colored sponges

scissors

indelible marker

Building Blocks

This activity encourages babies to develop basic number schemes and to recognize the relevant vocabulary.

Partially fill the bathtub or shallow basin with water. Cut the sponges into fish shapes or simply use the marker to draw fish shapes on the sponges. Place the sponges in the bathtub or basin and encourage the baby to play with them as they float on the water. Supervise carefully and make sure the baby doesn't chew off small pieces of the sponges. As he plays, talk to him about the colors, numbers, and sizes. For example, "That is a green fish. It is a little green fish. Can we find a big green fish?" or "That is a yellow fish. How many yellow fish are there? Let's count. There's one, two, three, four yellow fish!" Always begin your comments and questions by talking about the sponge the baby is focusing on at the moment, then expand and elaborate on whatever concepts are relevant.

Tunnel Crawl

What's at the end of the tunnel?
Some favorite people and things!

What You'll Need:

large cardboard box

assortment of favorite toys

After the baby has started crawling, remove the top and bottom flaps from a large box. Make sure there are no exposed metal staples or loose tape. Place the box on its side on the floor so that it makes a tunnel. Place the baby at one end of the tunnel. Briefly poke your head through the other end and say, "Where's Daddy?" or "Where's Mommy?" Pop your head in and out of the baby's sight and keep repeating the question, encouraging her to crawl through and find you. In addition or as an alternative, dangle some of the baby's favorite toys at the other end of the tunnel saying, "Where's the rattle?" or "Where's Teddy?" as appropriate. If the baby shows no interest in finding you or the toys, don't worry. Simply wait two or three weeks and then try this exercise again.

Building Blocks

This activity enhances gross motor abilities and encourages babies to use their understanding that objects exist even if they can't be seen.

Research indicates that children develop "object permanence" (they know something exists even if they can't see it) with people before they develop it with inanimate objects.

Buried Treasures

Now you see it; now you don't. Can baby find it?

What You'll Need:

small basin

uncooked oatmeal or quick oats

assortment of objects, such as a key ring, ball, plastic spoon

Fill the basin with the uncooked oatmeal or quick oats. Start by slipping your hand into the oats. Wiggle your fingers and ask the baby, "Where is my hand?" When he finds it, make sure to cheer, applaud, and say, "You found it!" Repeat a few times until the baby is comfortable finding your buried hand. Then take one of the items and bury it in the oats. The objects should be small enough to be easily grasped but too large to be swallowed. Make sure the baby sees you hiding the object. Ask him, "Where is the ball?" Repeat with the other objects. If the baby appears confused, allow part of each item to stick through the surface of the oats when you bury it. Then try the game again a week or two later with completely hidden objects.

Building Blocks

This activity stimulates memory and the use of mental imagery.

Name That Thing

Baby shows what she knows by pointing.

Note when the baby is alert but not involved in any particular activity. Ask, "Where is Daddy?" or "Where is the dog?" When she points correctly, provide lavish praise and applause. Start with things that are very familiar to the baby, then gradually increase the challenge. For example, ask, "Where is the television?" or "Where is the plate?" If the baby seems confused or frustrated, point to the item yourself and say, "There it is!" Then ask about the item again later. After a while, try introducing various adjectives along with the nouns. For example, ask, "Where is the blue cup?" or "Where is the big bowl?" Also try introducing parts of wholes. For example, ask "Where is the dog's tail?" or "Where are Daddy's shoes?"

Building Blocks

This activity enhances babies' ability to recognize and discriminate, as well as their capacity to use words to identify and differentiate objects and concepts.

Babies understand language sooner than they can speak, and their ability to understand increases more rapidly than does their ability to talk. Throughout early childhood, children can always understand much more than they can say.

Dump Truck

Filling or dumping—which does baby like better?

What You'll Need:

shoe boxes

---

assortment of small (but not small enough to be swallowed) objects, such as:

empty thread spools

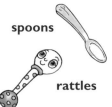
spoons

rattles

coasters

blocks

Sit on the floor with the baby. Demonstrate filling up the shoe box with the objects, then dumping them out. Encourage the baby to do the same. Talk to him about what is happening, saying, "All filled up" and "Now it's empty" as he plays. Use additional shoe boxes and objects to make different collections. Some can have mixtures of objects, while others can be sorted by kind. Each will look and sound different when baby fills and dumps out the box. As the baby fills the shoe boxes, provide appropriate commentary. For example, "It takes a lot of thread spools to fill up the box" or "We need more spoons to fill up the box." Expand and vary the exercise using boxes of different sizes. Make sure they are large enough that filling them is a bit of a challenge, but not so large that trying to dump them is frustrating.

Building Blocks

This activity refines large and small muscle skills while promoting the development of concepts relating to size, shape, and number.

Pitcher and Catcher

Do you have a budding pitcher or catcher? Baby tries out both roles with this ball game.

What You'll Need:

balls of different sizes

Make sure that none of the balls is small enough to be swallowed whole or fragile enough to be broken into small pieces. Sit on the floor with the baby and roll a ball to her. Encourage her to roll or throw it back. Comment on what is happening and on her performance. For example, "Here it comes!" or "There it goes!" and "Good catch!" or "Good throw!" Once the baby has become comfortable following and moving the ball, repeat the exercise with different balls. After that, try introducing new motions of various kinds such as "bouncers," "pop flies," and "spins." Introduce speed and pattern variations in small, gradual increments to avoid frustration, and use only soft balls to avoid injury. Also, allow the baby to see what happens when the balls are rolled or thrown on different surfaces, such as carpeting, hardwood, tile, or grass.

Building Blocks

This activity helps babies refine their large and small muscle skills, introduces them to properties of physical objects, and familiarizes them with basic social concepts such as taking turns.

Common Cause-and-Effects

*With the touch of a button or a flick of a switch,
baby learns how to make things work.*

What You'll Need:

**variety of household
appliances with buttons,
knobs, and switches**

Building Blocks

This activity helps
babies understand the
connection between
actions and their
consequences.

Carry the baby around the house. Demonstrate flicking on a light switch, pushing the buttons on the television remote control, turning the volume knob on the radio, and pressing the lever of the electric can opener. Encourage him to operate each of the mechanisms himself. If he has any difficulty (twisting and turning motions may be overly challenging for a while), place your hand on his and help him along. Talk to him about what he is doing. For example, "Pressing that button turns the television on and off" or "Turning that knob makes the radio louder." As long as it won't damage the mechanism, let him repeat the operations he finds particularly fascinating. Also, make sure that any appliances you do not want him to touch without supervision are kept well out of his reach.

Touch and Talk

What sound does the picture make?

What You'll Need:

several large pieces of cardboard

glue

pictures of things that make sounds (animals, bells, cars, horns) cut from magazines

Glue the pictures securely to the cardboard. When the glue is dry, place the cardboard in front of the baby. When she touches a picture, identify the object and make an appropriate sound. For instance, "That's a car—rmmm! rmmm!" or "That's a bell—ding dong, ding dong!" If the baby is particularly fascinated with certain pictures or is particularly delighted by certain sounds, encourage her to make the sound herself. If she has started speaking, encourage her to say the name as well. After a while, introduce new boards with specific themes, such as forms of transportation (car, truck, train) or zoo creatures (lion, elephant, gorilla). Use the baby's favorite pictures and sounds from the original board as a guide in creating the new theme boards.

Building Blocks

This activity enhances receptive and expressive language development while improving recognition and sorting skills.

Crunch, Throw, and Roll

Find out which kind of paper makes the best balls to throw and roll.

What You'll Need:

Several sheets of different kinds of papers of different sizes, such as:

tissue paper

wrapping paper

wax paper

notebook paper

construction paper

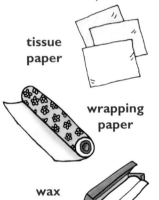

Crumple up one sheet of each kind of paper. Let the baby crumple up the others. Throw the crumpled-up balls of paper into the air and roll them along the floor. Encourage the baby to do the same. Describe the various properties of each kind of paper and what happens when the balls are thrown or rolled. Say, "That blue paper really flies when you throw it!" or "The wax paper doesn't roll very well." Let the baby tear the paper if he wants to, but make sure he doesn't ingest any of the pieces. Also, keep stationery, books, unread magazines and newspapers, or any other unsuitable paper products out of the baby's reach so his crumpling and tearing does not become inappropriate.

Building Blocks

This activity enhances motor skills and promotes awareness of cause and effect.

Sink or Swim

Baby discovers which objects float and which objects sink to the bottom of the tub.

What You'll Need:

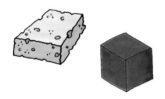

assortment of objects that float, such as sponges and wood blocks

assortment of objects that don't float, such as toy cars and metal spoons

Building Blocks

This activity increases awareness of the physical properties of objects and promotes the development of classification schemes.

Place the baby in a bathtub filled waist-high with water. Take various objects and drop them into the water in turn. Make sure the object has captured the baby's attention before you let it go, and make sure it falls directly in front of her. Before dropping each object ask, "Will it swim?" After the object is dropped, playfully exclaim, "Yesss!" if it floats or "Nooo!" if it doesn't. After all the items have been dropped, collect them and repeat the exercise. This time drop the items into the water from a greater height, but avoid splashing water in the baby's eyes. Add descriptions of the different splashes they make along with the "sink or swim" comments. If she shows interest, encourage the baby to pick up and drop the objects herself.

Two-Hand Monty

Gone but not forgotten? Which hand is hiding the toy?

What You'll Need:

small favorite toy

Building Blocks

This activity promotes improvements in the baby's capacity to deal with objects that can't immediately be seen or touched.

Hold the toy in front of the baby so that it captures his attention. Then place the toy in one of your hands, close both your hands into fists, and present the closed fists to the baby. Do this directly in front of the baby. Do not place your hands behind your back. Ask, "Where did it go?" If the baby shows no interest in looking for the toy, don't worry. Simply try again two or three weeks later. Once the baby does start looking for the toy, watch his reaction carefully. If he seems confused, open your hands immediately and show him the toy, then close your hands again. As he gets better at finding the toy, hold your fists closed for slightly longer periods of time.

Progressive Pouring

Baby discovers that big cups hold more than small ones.

What You'll Need:

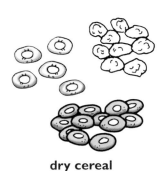

**paper cups of
different sizes**

dry cereal

Building Blocks

This activity helps refine hand-eye coordination and promotes the development of sequencing schemes.

Sit on the floor with the baby. Pour enough cereal into the smallest cup so it is almost filled. Demonstrate pouring the cereal from that cup into the next largest cup, and then the next. Let her look into each cup to see how much or how little it has been filled before moving on to the next. Reverse the process, pouring the cereal from the largest cup all the way back into the smallest. Again, let the baby look into each cup as you go. Encourage her to try the sequential pouring herself. Then fill several smaller cups and use them to fill the largest cup. Demonstrate what happens when the cereal is poured back into a smaller cup. Encourage the baby to try this as well. Also, give her the opportunity to nest the cups one inside the other when they are empty.

The "stranger anxiety" exhibited by many babies during the second half of the first year is not really an indication that they are afraid of people. Instead, it is a reflection of their temporary need to focus on close family members while they learn the basics of social interaction.

Hide, Find, and Hug

Find Mom or Dad and get a great, big hug!

What You'll Need:

safe open area with a variety of furniture, pillows, or cushions

large cardboard boxes

Building Blocks

This activity allows babies to improve their capacity to form and hold mental images of things that can no longer be seen or heard.

Hide from the baby. Call out, "Where am I?" and "Come and get me!" When the baby finds you, reward her with a big hug. Then hide again. Start with places where you are only partially hidden, such as behind a chair or table. Gradually make the game more challenging by hiding more completely behind a stack of cushions or boxes. Watch the baby carefully. If she shows signs of frustration, reveal yourself immediately and then drop out of sight again. Also, if the baby indicates an interest in reversing the exercise, either by hiding herself or simply moving away from you, play along. Say, "Where are you?" and "I'm coming to get you!" and then give her a big hug when you find her.

See and Squish

Plastic bags filled with paint let baby smoosh colors without making a mess.

What You'll Need:

**reclosable plastic
sandwich bags**

spoon

**non-toxic
tempera paints**

tape

Building Blocks

This activity enhances tactile awareness and helps babies begin developing basic sorting schemes.

Place several spoonfuls of paint into a reclosable plastic sandwich bag. Seal the bag and secure the closure with tape. Place the bag in front of the baby. Demonstrate pressing it and squeezing it, encouraging the baby to do the same. As she handles the bag and looks at the paint, describe what she is feeling and seeing, saying, "That is red paint. It feels soft and squishy when you squeeze it." Repeat the process using different colors of paint. Watch for leaks or tears in the bags. Allow the baby to play with each one separately, and then place several different bags in front of her simultaneously. In addition, place spoonfuls of two or three different colors of paints into one bag. As the baby handles the bag and the colors mix together, describe what's happening by saying, "Look at the colors swirl together. Mixing blue and yellow together made green!"

Container & Cover Challenge

Sorting becomes more challenging with real pots and containers.

What You'll Need:

assortment of plastic tubs with lids and metal pots with covers

Surround the baby with the tubs, lids, pots, and covers. Make sure that each lid or cover is light enough to be handled easily. The pot covers should have knobs that make them easy for little fingers to grasp. Demonstrate placing the covers on the appropriate containers and encourage the baby to do so as well. Describe what he's doing, saying, "That's too big" or "That's too small" and "That's just right!" as appropriate. Don't worry if the baby seems to have a lot of trouble matching the right covers and bottoms. At first, he probably will use simple "trial and error." But as the weeks go on and he becomes familiar with the materials, his selections gradually will become more purposeful and accurate.

Building Blocks

This activity enhances small muscle abilities and stimulates the development of sorting skills.

Mountain Climbing

Bring your baby to new heights by making this mini Alps.

What You'll Need:

**collection of
large cushions**

Building Blocks

This activity promotes
the development of
gross motor skills
and stimulates
problem solving.

*Some children skip
crawling and go right
to walking. Although
some parents worry
about this unusual pat-
tern of development,
there is no evidence
that it results in
learning disabilities or
any long-term problems
whatsoever.*

Place one cushion on the floor. Stack two cushions next to it, then stack three cushions next to those. Place the baby in front of the first cushion and encourage her to climb. Make sure to hold the cushions firmly in place as she attempts to get to each level. Use a free hand to guide her and keep her from wandering off to either side. Provide enthusiastic cheering for the baby's efforts and plenty of kisses whenever she reaches a new plateau. Once the baby has climbed to the top, hold her gently but securely and "slide" her back down the mountain. A loud "Wheeeee!" from you will make the ride even more fun. If the baby shows no inclination to climb or has significant difficulty climbing, don't worry. Simply play the sliding game and then try the climbing part a few weeks later.

Chapter 4
12 to 18 Months

During the first half of their second year, babies become bold adventurers. They crawl, climb, and walk wherever they can. They use their more refined senses and fine motor movements to thoroughly examine everything they encounter. They are fascinated by how things work, and they are eager to perform "experiments" by applying their skills and interacting with materials in new and different ways. The receptive vocabulary (words they understand) of babies in this age group expands enormously, and they may start to talk. Their capacity to form mental images improves, and they begin to use this ability to make sense of the world and to organize and store information for later use.

Body Art

Who needs a brush when you've got feet to paint with?

What You'll Need:

 old newspapers

 cardboard boxes

 plastic trays or basin

 nontoxic tempera or water color paints

 large sheets of paper

 bowl of water

 paper towels

Spread out the newspapers on the floor. Cover a wide area, and use several layers of newspaper to protect the floor. Place the cardboard boxes around the newspaper to create a barricade that will help keep the baby from wandering off the newspapers. Pour a little paint into a plastic tray, and pour other colors into separate trays. Place a piece of paper in the middle of the newspapers. Let the baby stand in the tray and then walk across the paper. If the baby is not yet walking, let him put his hands in the trays and then crawl across the paper. Keep a bowl of water and paper towels handy so you can rinse the paint off the baby's feet before changing colors and when he has finished creating his artwork. Display baby's creations in a place where he can see them easily and often.

Building Blocks

This activity enhances body awareness and nurtures the baby's emerging creativity.

Family Puzzles

It's a puzzlement! Can baby put faces and bodies back together again?

What You'll Need:

duplicate photographs of family members

index cards

glue

scissors

Glue each of the photographs to an index card. When the glue is dry, cut each of the cards into two pieces that are about the same size. Don't cut the photographs in front of the baby, as she may be frightened by seeing the faces and bodies being cut. Place all the halves in front of the baby and mix them up. Encourage her to put the appropriate pieces together. At first, it may be necessary to provide a little help. If the baby seems confused or frustrated, pick up a piece, show it to her, and ask, "Where is the rest of Daddy?" Start with just two photographs, then add a third and a fourth as the baby becomes more comfortable and adept at matching the pieces.

Building Blocks

This activity helps babies develop the perception of parts and wholes.

Tug-of-War

*Baby will be surprised at his own strength
when he pulls you over!*

What You'll Need:

scarf
or
towel

Building Blocks

This activity enhances gross motor development while stimulating language and social skills.

During the second year of life, children spend a great deal of time engaged in steady staring. Although they may appear to be doing nothing, they actually are very busy absorbing a wealth of new information with their eyes.

Hold one end of the scarf or towel and give the other end to the baby. Pull on it slowly and gently. Encourage the baby to pull back. Be patient. It may take a few tries before he stops letting go and catches on to the game. Entertain the baby with exaggerated grunts and groans along with corresponding facial expressions whenever he applies opposing force. Once he is comfortable with the tugging game, vary the speed and pressure of your pulls. Do so with enough force so that it creates a different "feel" for the baby, but don't use so much force that the scarf or towel is yanked out of his hand. As you alter the pattern of your pulls, describe the differences, using words such as "harder," "easier," "faster," and "slower."

Administrative Assistant

Let baby give you a hand with your piles of paperwork.

What You'll Need:

junk mail

scrap paper

old magazines

crayons

wastebasket

When doing simple home-office work, such as paying bills and opening the mail, let the baby "participate." While you work, encourage her to imitate you by tearing up the junk mail, scribbling on the scrap paper with crayons, and turning the pages of the magazines. Talk to the baby about what you both are doing. For example, say, "We're opening the mail" or "We're writing a letter." When you are done, invite the baby to help you clean up by throwing everything into the wastebasket. Make sure any materials that are unsafe or inappropriate for the baby to play with are kept out of her reach.

Building Blocks
This activity teaches babies about roles and routines and stimulates their imitative abilities.

Taking Turns

Here's a first lesson in give and take.

What You'll Need:

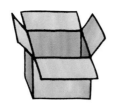

large cardboard box

favorite rattles, vehicles, and other toys

Building Blocks

This activity introduces babies to the concept of taking turns and helps them develop interpersonal skills.

Place all the toys in the cardboard box. Sit on the floor with the baby. Take one toy out of the box, hand it to the baby, and say, "Your turn." Count to three out loud, then take the toy back and say, "My turn." Repeat the exercise with all of the toys, taking them out of the box and replacing them one at a time so as not to distract the baby with too many items. Make sure you keep your voice playful and upbeat, conveying the impression that sharing is fun. If the baby seems comfortable with the process, gradually increase the length of time you each hold the toy by counting to four, then five. If the baby seems distressed when a toy is taken away, reduce the count and hand the toy back to him more quickly.

Size of the Splash

Drop objects into the tub and see how much they splash!

What You'll Need:

variety of objects, such as:

empty plastic bottles

soap bars

plastic toys

key rings

blocks

small footstool

Building Blocks

This activity promotes the formation of concepts relating to actions and their consequences and stimulates the development of classification schemes.

Let the baby stand next to a bathtub filled with water, and ask her to drop the various objects into the water one at a time. Comment on the different splashes they make and what happens to them when they hit the water. For example, say, "That made a big splash, then it sank!" or "That didn't make such a big splash, but look, it's floating." Retrieve the objects and let the baby repeat the splashes she found particularly interesting or entertaining. Retrieve the objects again. Then place the footstool next to the tub. Allow the baby to stand on the footstool, and hold her securely. Encourage her to drop the objects again, but this time from a greater height. (It is not safe to allow the baby to stand on the edge of the bathtub.)

Riding the Wind

Baby's breath is the fuel that makes these objects fly.

What You'll Need:

assortment of light objects, such as:

feather

Ping-Pong ball

cotton ball

balloon

box

Place the objects on the floor. Kneel down and make each object "fly" in turn by blowing at it repeatedly. Let the baby chase and retrieve the objects. Then encourage him to make each of the objects fly himself. Always provide careful supervision, as these items may break or come apart and the baby might try to put the pieces in his mouth. After the baby has become adept at making the objects fly around wildly, make the game more challenging. Sit across from the baby, blow an object directly toward him, then encourage him to blow it directly back to you. Or place a box on its side on the floor, demonstrate blowing an object into the box, and encourage the baby to do the same.

Building Blocks

This activity helps babies understand the connection between their actions and the consequences of them. It also stimulates the development of problem-solving skills.

After their first birthday, children increasingly engage in "deferred imitation." They will continue to mimic actions immediately but will also mimic actions they have seen minutes, hours, and even days earlier.

A World of Smells

Baby's nose knows what smells good and what doesn't.

What You'll Need:

 empty spice containers with shaker tops

 glue

---

assortment of "smelly" materials, such as:

 cotton ball soaked in perfume

 whole cloves

 orange peel

 pieces of onion or garlic

Place each of the materials in a different container. Secure the lids with glue so they can't be pulled off. Pick up a container and describe what you smell. For example, say, "This smells like a flower, how nice!" or "This smells like something we like to eat!" Encourage the baby to pick up the containers and smell them, too. Identify what she is smelling. Mimic her reactions in addition to describing them. Next, select 3 or 4 containers that elicited particularly strong reactions. Place them in front of the baby and ask, "Can you give me something that smells delicious?" or "Can you give me something that smells stinky?" Let the baby carry around any containers that she likes, and encourage her to share the smells with other family members.

Building Blocks

This activity refines the baby's sensory discrimination skills and stimulates language learning.

Picture Book Theater

Mom and Dad make books come alive.

What You'll Need:

favorite picture books

Building Blocks

This activity stimulates imagination and promotes the development of basic literacy concepts.

Children's first "active" interest in books usually is not associated with reading. At about one year of age, they become fascinated with simple mechanisms, such as the hinges of a book binding. They often will turn one page back and forth several times before moving on to the next page.

Encourage the baby to turn the pages of his favorite picture book. Identify whatever he sees, and tell a "story" to go along with the pictures. Be as creative and entertaining as possible. Give the various characters different voices and use exaggerated movements to act out scenes and situations. Involve the baby in the action as well by asking him questions relating to the pictures in the book. For example, if it is an alphabet picture book with "A is for Apple" and "L is for Lion," crawl around on all fours, throw back your head and roar loudly, and then say, "I'm a lion prowling through the jungle and I am very hungry. Can you find something for me to eat in that book?"

Play Dough Patterns

Pinch, poke, and roll this favorite dough.

What You'll Need:

bowl

flour

salt

water

food coloring

spoon

cup

In a large bowl, knead together 1 cup flour, ½ cup salt, and enough water (about ½ cup) to make no-cook play dough. Use a few drops of different food coloring in each batch to create an eye-pleasing assortment. If the baby shows interest, allow her to help by squishing the ingredients together. When it is fully prepared, let the baby pat, poke, pinch, and punch the play dough. Show her how to roll it into a ball, and then press it flat or roll it into a long tube. Encourage her to do the same. In addition, use cups, spoons, and other such items to make interesting shapes. Cookie cutters may be included, too, but the baby should use these only with careful supervision.

Building Blocks

This activity promotes tactile awareness and introduces babies to the concept of transformation.

Indoor Sports

Transform everyday items into sports equipment and have a ball!

What You'll Need:

old newspaper

masking tape

empty paper towel rolls

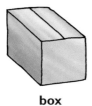

box

Building Blocks

This activity refines large muscle skills and stimulates the imagination.

Find or create an open area in the home. Crunch the newspaper into a big ball, then wrap the masking tape around it securely so it keeps its shape. Show the baby how to use the paper towel rolls as a bat or club to safely play "baseball" or "golf" indoors. Encourage the baby to hit the ball himself, and make sure to cheer and applaud enthusiastically whenever he makes contact with the ball. As the baby becomes more adept at making contact, try increasing the challenge. Pitch the ball to him by rolling it slowly along the floor. Or place a large empty box on its side on the floor and encourage the baby to hit the ball into it. Provide a running commentary, saying, "Home run!" or "Hole in one!" as appropriate.

Kid-Friendly Kaleidoscopes

Watch colors swirl and bubble when you roll these bottles.

What You'll Need:

 small, empty, clear plastic pop bottles

 water

 vegetable oil

food coloring

 glue

 eyedropper

Fill a bottle about ⅔ full with water. Add 3 tablespoons of vegetable oil and a few drops of food coloring. Glue the cap onto the bottle securely. When the glue is dry, demonstrate shaking the bottle and rolling it on the floor, then let the baby shake the bottle and roll it on the floor. Talk to her about the interesting bubbles and waves she creates by moving the bottle around. Create other bottles using different colors and combinations of colors. If the baby shows interest in helping to make the kaleidoscope, let her use an eyedropper to add the colors of her choice. If the baby is particularly enthralled with rolling the bottles on the floor, use 2-liter pop bottles to create even larger kaleidoscopes.

Building Blocks

This activity promotes visual awareness and stimulates the development of concepts relating to motion.

Waterfall Wonders

It's raining, it's pouring—in the tub!

What You'll Need:

hammer and nail

disposable plastic containers and bottles

Use the hammer and nail to make holes in the bottoms of the containers and bottles. Vary the number and size of the holes for each one. When the baby is in the bath, scoop up water with each container and hold it high over him. Describe the number and size of the streams of water that come cascading down. Let the water fall onto the baby's head, face, and hands. If he is uncomfortable being "showered" in this way, simply have the streams trickle down into the water around him. Scoop up more water and encourage the baby to hold some of the smaller containers or bottles himself. And if he shows an interest, help him hold up the heavier ones, too.

Building Blocks

This activity stimulates the development of basic concepts and classification schemes relating to number and size.

Verbal Gymnastics

Simon Says—in two parts.

What You'll Need:

small assortment of favorite toys

Building Blocks

This activity expands vocabulary and stimulates the development of sequencing skills.

Before they are 1¹/₂ to 2 years of age, children tend to reserve their "sociability" primarily for adults. They often treat other children more like inanimate objects instead of living beings.

Hand the baby a toy. Give her a simple instruction, such as "Put the doll on my head." Follow that with another instruction, such as "Hide the doll behind the sofa." After a while, increase the complexity of the instructions. For instance, give the baby two toys and two instructions, such as "Put the rattle on the table, and hide the block under the chair." Use as many "directional" adjectives as you can: over and under, in front of and behind, at the top and at the bottom, inside and outside, etc. If the baby seems confused after completing the first of the two instructions, repeat the second one. Then give another two-part instruction, and encourage her to try again. Make sure to cheer and applaud when she completes any instruction and to cheer and applaud extra loud when she completes a combination of instructions.

Share and Share Alike

It's a big deal when baby learns to share.

What You'll Need:

 large cookie broken into small pieces

or

small pile of easy-to-handle dry cereal

Building Blocks

This activity enhances interpersonal skills and promotes the development of number concepts.

Children learn a lot by exploring and investigating on their own. Making your home as safe and accessible as possible provides the best learning environment—one that minimizes the need to constantly say, "no," "stop," and "don't touch."

Place the cookie pieces or cereal bits in front of the baby. Ask him, "May I please have one?" Wait for the baby to pick up a piece and offer it to you. When he does, react with exaggerated delight, thank him, and then ask, "May I please have some more?" Let the baby decide how much "more" is. Then reverse roles. Put all the pieces back into a pile and ask, "Would you like one?" and "Would you like some more?" If the baby is more interested in eating than sharing, try the game later, substituting small blocks for the food. Also, once the baby becomes comfortable with the sharing process, make the game a little more sophisticated. Ask, "Would you like to have two?" and "Would you like to have three?"

Staircase Avalanche

Look out below!

What You'll Need:

flight of stairs

assortment of balls

Place the baby in a comfortable position at the bottom of the stairs. Sit just a few stairs up (so you are readily available to supervise and guide him if he decides to start climbing). Roll each ball down the stairs in turn. Be patient and wait between each roll until you have the baby's attention again. He may need a few seconds to watch each ball roll along the floor at the bottom of the stairs, too. Talk about the different sights and sounds created by each ball. Retrieve the balls, and then roll them down the stairs two at a time. Retrieve the balls again, and then roll them down the stairs all at once. Invite the baby to sit in your lap. Hold him securely, and let him roll some himself. Take him all the way to the top of the stairs, hold him securely, and let him roll the balls from there.

Clothespin Challenge

Here's a baby-oriented version of the clothespin-in-a-bottle game.

What You'll Need:

slender wooden or plastic clothespins

clean, empty 2-liter soda-pop bottle

Building Blocks

This activity promotes the development of small muscle skills and increases number awareness.

Make sure the clothespins do not have "squeeze" mechanisms that might pinch little fingers and that the pop bottle is clean and dry. Show the baby how to put a clothespin into the bottle. Encourage him to fill the bottle with clothespins. As he puts them in, count "One, two, three" out loud. When the bottle is full, let the baby shake it and listen to the noise. Then ask him to empty the bottle. Getting the clothespins into the bottle is fun and challenging, but getting them back out is harder. If the baby shows any signs of frustration, substitute a wide-mouth juice bottle. After the baby has mastered filling and emptying the juice bottle, try using the pop bottle at a later time.

Reflective Dance Recital

Look at me dance!

What You'll Need:

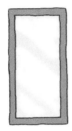

full-length mirror

**CD or
cassette tape player**

**favorite songs of
different tempos**

Building Blocks

This activity refines motor skills, increases body awareness, and promotes the development of classification schemes.

Stand the baby in front of a full-length mirror that is well-secured to a wall or door. Play one of her favorite songs. Encourage her to dance to the music and to watch herself while she dances. Cheer the baby on, and join her in the dance if you feel so inclined. Play different tunes, and give the baby a chance to dance differently. If she repeats essentially the same motions, demonstrate some changes that reflect the new tempo. As the baby creates a new dance or imitates you, talk to her about what you both are doing. For example, "This is a slow one, we're swaying gently back and forth," or "This is a lively tune, we're bouncing up and down." Try playing some of your favorite popular or classical selections as well.

Personalized Picture Book

Build a library of books depicting baby's favorite people and things.

What You'll Need:

 glue

family photographs and/or pictures of favorite objects cut from magazines

several pieces of cardboard

 **hole punch**

yarn

Building Blocks
This activity enhances fine motor abilities and stimulates the development of basic literacy concepts.

Glue the photographs and/or pictures securely to pieces of cardboard. When the glue is dry, punch holes in the left side of the cardboard. Thread the yarn through the holes and tie a bow to hold the pieces together. Invite the baby to "read" the book you have created. Describe what he sees when he turns the pages. Put together a "series" of such books devoted to different themes. For example, "Our Family," "Your Favorite Playthings," "Our House and Neighborhood," etc. Remember to be patient. At first, the baby may be enthralled with just turning a single page back and forth and show no interest in proceeding forward. Let him do so for a while, and then gently encourage him to "see what's next."

Little Squirt, Big Squirt

Bottles that spray and squirt make bath time an adventure.

What You'll Need:

assortment of clean, empty, plastic liquid containers that spray or squirt when squeezed

Building Blocks

This activity promotes fine motor skills and enhances the development of cause-and-effect concepts.

Collect empty containers of perfume, cleansers, mustard, ketchup, and anything else that sprays or squirts liquids. Make sure all the containers are unbreakable and have been thoroughly cleaned, leaving no trace of any substance that may be toxic. Also, make sure the spray or squirt mechanisms are easy to operate. Fill the containers about halfway with water so they still float. Place the containers in the bathtub. Demonstrate to the baby how each one works. Talk to the baby about the different types of mechanisms and the different sprays or squirts they make. Encourage the baby to use each of the containers herself. Once she is comfortable operating the various mechanisms and has observed the sprays or squirts they make, provide a few floating objects (toy boat, soap bar, sponge) to use as targets.

Supermarket Sweeps

Baby shops and checks out at your living-room grocery.

What You'll Need:

assortment of light canned and paper goods

plastic "play" foods

small basket or small plastic shopping cart

calculator

grocery bags

Building Blocks

This activity promotes creativity and expands receptive and expressive vocabulary.

Place the canned and paper goods and the plastic play food all around the room. Use the edge of a sofa, a coffee table, low shelves, and any other areas that give the baby easy access to the items. Give the baby the basket or cart and encourage him to go "shopping." Follow him around and talk to him about his selections. For example, "Yes, we need more paper towels!" or "Tuna fish is a good choice; we can make sandwiches for lunch!" When the baby has filled the basket, use the calculator to set up a pretend checkout station. Ring up each of the baby's purchases and place them in the grocery bags. If the baby shows interest, replace all the items and reverse roles. Do a quick "shopping" and then let him operate the "cash register" and pack the bags.

Action Photos

Your fingers make photographs come alive.

What You'll Need:

duplicate family photographs

scissors

glue

index cards

hole punch

Find some full-body photographs of family members. Cut off the arms or the legs. (Do the cutting out of the baby's sight to avoid frightening her.) Glue the photographs securely to index cards. When the glue is dry, punch holes where the arms or legs should be. Stick your fingers through the holes and use them as arms or legs to create "action" figures. As you entertain the baby, talk about what you are doing. For example, "Look, Daddy is running" or "Mommy is waving bye-bye." Encourage the baby to stick her fingers through the holes and create action figures, too. In addition or as an alternative, use pictures cut from magazines. Animals can be included, substituting fingers from both hands for all four legs and for antlers or horns.

Building Blocks

This activity promotes imagination and enhances receptive and expressive language development.

Chapter 5
18 to 24 Months

While action dominated the first half of the second year, toddlers between 18 and 24 months become "thinkers." Their mental images are strong and stable enough for them to organize and store experiences more effectively. As a result, they no longer live primarily in the present, and they routinely "use their head" to solve problems. Toddlers at this age also show signs of imagination and creativity, coming up with their own ideas and then expressing them through their ever-improving physical skills. As their capacity to understand and use language steadily increases, they will start to actively construct and refine concepts that will become the foundation for later literacy and numerical skills.

Alternative Art Canvas

Create a variety of effects by drawing on different materials.

What You'll Need:

sheets of various materials such as:

construction paper

brown paper bags

cardboard

aluminum foil and wax paper

tissue paper

crayons

paints (tempera, watercolor) and paintbrush

Lay out sheets of different materials on a table. Encourage the toddler to draw or scribble on each one. Talk to the toddler about the feel and appearance of each one. For example, say, "That makes an interesting picture when you draw on the shiny aluminum foil!" or "The wax paper doesn't work very well as something to scribble on, even when you press hard, does it?" Ask the toddler which effects she likes best and give her additional sheets of the materials that produce those effects. In addition, invite the toddler to use paints on the materials. Talk about the different looks and textures produced by tempera paints and watercolor paints. Display the artwork in an area where the toddler can admire it easily and often.

Building Blocks

This activity stimulates imagination and promotes the development of classification schemes.

Ice Cube Surprises

Watch the cubes melt and see what they reveal!

What You'll Need:

ice cube tray

 food coloring

assortment of small objects such as:

 coins

buttons

 paper clips

clear plastic storage bag

 masking tape

Pour water into an ice cube tray. Add different food coloring to each section, using enough to make the water fairly dark. Place a different item in each section and then put the tray in the freezer. When the cubes are frozen, remove them from the tray and put them into a large clear plastic bag. Seal the bag securely with masking tape. Let the toddler handle the bag. Encourage him to count the total number of cubes and the number of cubes of each color. Describe what is happening as the ice melts and the colors mix together. Ask him to find and identify the various items as they gradually appear. When all the ice is fully melted, encourage the toddler to count the total number of items in the bag and the number of each kind of item.

Building Blocks

This activity enhances the development of number concepts and sorting skills.

Animal Acts

Guess which animal Mom or Dad is pretending to be.

Pretend to be different animals that the toddler is familiar with. Get down on all fours and bark like a dog. Curl up in a ball and meow like a cat. Hop around the room like a kangaroo. Rear up and roar like a lion. Gallop along the floor like a horse. Challenge the toddler to figure out what animal you are. If she has a little difficulty, provide a few hints. For example, "A cowboy is riding me to town" or "I'm the king of the jungle." Invite the toddler to switch roles. As she acts out different animals, pretend to be stumped for a while. Instead of guessing right away, ask her to give you some hints, either verbally or through additional actions.

Building Blocks

This activity will stimulate creativity and the development of problem-solving skills and classification schemes.

Young children have a tendency to focus on beginning and end states while ignoring "transformations." For example, when they see an adult put on a scary mask, they may become easily frightened because they see the person and the monster, but they do not process the person "becoming" the monster.

Peanut Butter Construction

Your junior architect constructs his own edible edifices.

What You'll Need:

clean tray or plate

plastic knife

peanut butter

crackers

marshmallows

pretzel rods

With a plastic knife, spread some peanut butter on a tray or plate. Demonstrate how to build "walls" by sticking crackers vertically in the peanut butter. Spread a little peanut butter along the top of the crackers and demonstrate how to add a roof by placing more crackers horizontally or at an angle on top. Encourage the toddler to create other structures, using the crackers as "bricks" and the peanut butter as "mortar." In addition, invite him to use other foods to add features to the buildings and the "neighborhood." Marshmallows can be bushes, and pretzel rods can be trees. Let the toddler play with his creations for a while, and then permit him to eat all or part of them, as appropriate.

Building Blocks

This activity helps develop coordination, problem-solving skills, and imagination.

Imaginative Props

Here's how to talk on a banana or put lipstick on with a pickle.

What You'll Need:

assortment of real or toy items such as:

telephone

lipstick

cookie

---

plus corresponding props such as:

banana

pickle

coaster

Show the toddler the real items. Then use the props to pursue a make-believe activity. For example, hold the banana like a telephone receiver and have a pretend conversation or pick up the coaster and pretend to nibble on it. Encourage the toddler to pick up a "real" item and mimic you or join you in the activity. Do not tell her which item to choose. Give her a chance to select the appropriate one herself. After going through all the items, place the make-believe ones in front of the toddler and encourage her to use them as props in similar activities or activities of her own creation. When she does, select the appropriate "real" item and mimic or join her.

Building Blocks

This activity stimulates creativity and enhances representational thinking.

Stop and Go

Whether you're going fast or slow, you'll have to freeze on command.

Use any tune you like to sing a variety of movement commands to the toddler. For example, "Spin, spin, spin!" or "Jump, jump, jump!" Model the appropriate action and encourage the toddler to mimic you. Once he becomes comfortable with the movements, occasionally "freeze" and call out "Stop!" After the toddler has "frozen," too, call out "Go!" and resume your movement. You can also introduce variations in speed. For example, "wiggle, wiggle, wiggle, slower, slower, slower" or "run, run, run, faster, faster, faster." Also, try introducing combinations of movements, such as "hop and turn, hop and turn." If the toddler shows interest in reversing roles, permit him to be the leader and follow whatever commands he gives. If he simply models the commands without saying them, say the appropriate words for him as you do whatever he is doing.

Girls used to be more advanced than boys in fine motor skills, and boys used to be more advanced than girls in gross motor skills. However, in recent years, as parents have been providing their male and female children with more equivalent types of play experiences, these differences have been disappearing.

Building Blocks

This activity helps develop body control and large muscle skills, and it promotes listening skills.

Imitation Station

It's a game to copy and be copied.

Stand or sit in front of the toddler. Whenever she does or says something, imitate her actions and vocalizations with an exaggerated flair. She probably will be highly amused and will start experimenting with all sorts of movements and sounds. (If, on the other hand, she appears to be annoyed by this activity at the moment, cease immediately and then try it again a day or two later.) If and when the toddler tires of being the leader, invite her to switch roles. Make silly motions and noises and encourage her to mimic you. Again, use exaggeration to provide a vivid model, and go slowly so she has a chance to figure out precisely how to copy you. Then find another family member (or even the family pet) so you and the toddler can both imitate the movements and sounds.

Building Blocks

This activity promotes interpersonal awareness and stimulates imagination.

Many children who are developing superb language skills may not start speaking until they are almost two years old—and then they may start speaking in complete sentences.

Archeology for Beginners

Follow the map to uncover the buried treasures.

What You'll Need:

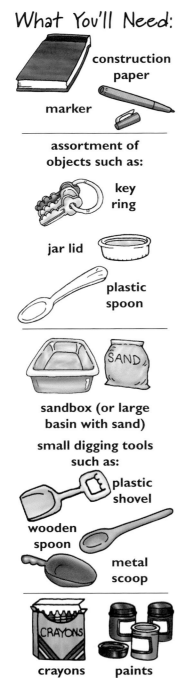

construction paper

marker

assortment of objects such as:

key ring

jar lid

plastic spoon

sandbox (or large basin with sand)

small digging tools such as:

plastic shovel

wooden spoon

metal scoop

crayons

paints

Create an archeological "chart" by tracing the outline of each object on the construction paper with the marker. Place the chart next to the sandbox. Bury all of the objects in the sand. Challenge the toddler to find each object and then put it in the appropriate place on the chart. Talk to him as he does so, identifying each object he finds. For example, "You found the key ring! Where does it go?" If he's interested, give him an opportunity to play with the digging tools and objects in the sand for a while. Then repeat the exercise, burying the objects in different places. Afterwards, allow the toddler to use his crayons or paints to color in the out-line of each of the objects on the chart.

Building Blocks

This activity stimulates memory skills and pattern recognition.

Garden Hose Symphony

Everyday items are the instruments in this backyard orchestra.

What You'll Need:

assortment of metal pots, pans, pie tins

garden hose with spray nozzle

Building Blocks

This activity stimulates creative expression and expands the understanding of cause-and-effect.

Arrange the pots, pans, and tins in a row. Turn on the hose, and demonstrate how to operate the nozzle. Make "music" by spraying the different items. Hand the nozzle to the toddler and encourage her to make music, too. If the nozzle can be adjusted, let her try making different kinds of music by changing the spray. Once the toddler has become adept at operating the nozzle, add some other items. A metal rake, an empty plastic garbage pail, a paper bag, and other items can be used to increase the size and variety of the outdoor "orchestra." Invite the toddler to sing her favorite songs as she conducts the orchestra, and encourage her to make up new tunes to go along with the sounds she is making.

Taste Detective

Don't look—let other senses be the guide.

What You'll Need:

blindfold

variety of favorite and other foods with distinctive flavors, odors, and textures

Building Blocks

This activity helps refine sensory abilities and promotes problem-solving.

Blindfold the toddler, making sure the blindfold is comfortable yet tight enough to discourage peeking. Place a piece of one of the toddler's favorite foods in his hand and ask him to identify it by using his senses of touch, smell, and taste. Repeat with pieces of other favorite foods. Next, introduce pieces of foods the toddler has not eaten before. When he is stumped, tell him the name of the food while lifting the blindfold and letting him look at it as well. Play the game again later, mixing in any of the new foods he likes with an assortment of his old favorites. Occasionally try slipping in some nutritious food the toddler says he doesn't like—he may be surprised to find that he likes it.

Imaginary Hospital

Playing doctor to Teddy helps prepare for future illnesses.

What You'll Need:

stuffed animals or dolls

---

medical supplies such as:

thermometer

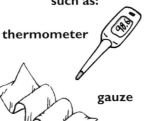

gauze

adhesive bandages

syringe substitute (eyedropper or turkey baster)

Make up a story about a stuffed animal or doll having a minor ailment. Encourage the toddler to play "doctor." Talk to her about what will help cure the ailment and why. Start with stories about illnesses or accidents the toddler has experienced herself. Then introduce those that you anticipate may occur in the near future. Emphasize the role of a good patient as well as the role of the doctor. Make sure to keep the stories reassuring and avoid anything that might unduly frighten the toddler. Always end the activity in a positive manner, saying, "You made it all better!" or "OK, let him get some rest, and I'll bet he'll be back in tip-top shape in no time!" In addition, tell the toddler that a particular stuffed animal or doll needs a routine check-up. Then help her carry out the procedures of a regular examination.

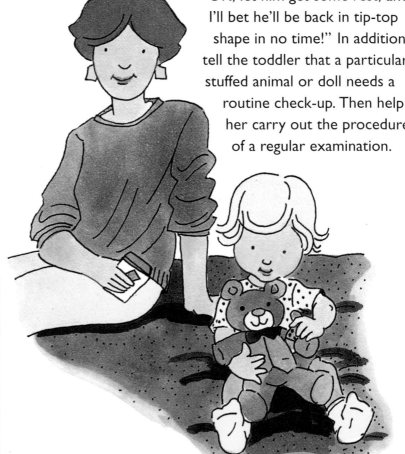

Building Blocks

This activity provides preparation for special situations and stimulates the development of empathy.

Purposeful Mistakes

When Mom and Dad are wrong,
toddlers love to correct them!

Make believe you don't know what simple things are or how to do simple routines. For example, point to the toddler's nose and ask, "Is this your mouth?" Try to put the toddler's shoes on his hands. Hold a book upside down and flip through the pages. Let the toddler get a kick out of correcting you. If he simply indicates that you are incorrect, do not correct yourself right away. For instance, if he just says "no" when you point to his nose and ask, "Is this your mouth?" say, "Is it your chin? Your belly button? Your eyes?" Or, if he merely pulls his hands away when you attempt to put the shoes on them, try to put them on top of his head or on his ears. Keep going with "wrong" answers or activities until he correctly identifies the object or demonstrates the activity.

Building Blocks

This activity promotes concept formation and enhances the ability to sense discrepancies.

Obstacle Course Adventure

Over, under, around, and through...
an obstacle course just for you.

What You'll Need:

assortment of large household items and furniture, such as:

pillows

cushions

boxes

chairs

tables

Use several items to create an indoor obstacle course. Encourage the toddler to follow you as you negotiate your way through the course. Describe what you are doing as you go. Use as many action and directional words as you can. For example, say, "We are climbing over the pillow, we are crawling under the table, we are walking around the chair, or we are tiptoeing behind the box." Go through the obstacle course again, this time altering the pattern. For example, say, "This time, we are running in front of the chair, pushing away the box, jumping on top of the pillow, and rolling under the table." Reverse roles. Encourage the toddler to take the lead and describe the pattern she chooses to pursue as you follow her through the course.

Building Blocks

This activity enhances large motor skills and stimulates the development of linguistic concepts.

Edible Arithmetic

Counting and sorting never tasted so good!

What You'll Need:

large bag of M&M's

clean table surface

Building Blocks

This activity enhances discrimination skills and stimulates the development of various number concepts.

Pour out the M&M's onto the table, and have the toddler assist you in sorting them into piles by color. Ask the toddler which pile he thinks has the most pieces and which he thinks has the fewest. Then ask him to help you lay out all the piles of M&M's in rows. Make sure you maintain a one-to-one pattern across the rows as you do so. Help the toddler count the number of M&M's in each row. Point to two rows at a time and help the toddler count how many more pieces there are in the longer row. Let the toddler do whatever M&M eating is necessary to make all of the rows even. Then help him count the number of pieces in each row again.

Shadowy Figures

Cast a shadow, then fill it in!

What You'll Need:

large sheets of butcher paper

crayons
or

markers
or

paints and paintbrush

Building Blocks

This activity enhances understanding of the physical world and stimulates imagination.

Find an open area outside on a day that the sun is shining brightly or darken a room and turn on a lamp so that vivid shadows are created. Lay out a sheet of butcher paper on the ground or on the floor. Show the toddler how you can project your own shadow onto the paper. Encourage her to stand so she can project her shadow onto the paper, helping her get into position if necessary. Ask her to hold still for a minute while you trace her shadow on the paper. Then invite her to move about and make shadows of different shapes on other pieces of paper. After several outlines have been created, let the toddler use her crayons, markers, or paints to fill in the figures.

Distance Volume Vocalizing

Louder or softer—it depends on how far away you are.

Ask the toddler to sing a favorite song that involves some sort of transportation, such as "The Wheels on the Bus" or "Yankee Doodle." Sing along with him, and pretend you are the bus or the pony. As you move farther away, gradually lower your voice until it is a barely audible whisper. As you get closer, gradually make your voice louder until you are almost shouting. Talk to the toddler about the relationship between distance and volume. Then encourage him to play the part of the bus or pony and alter his voice as he drives or rides back and forth. Be prepared to supply a little guidance at first, saying, "softer, softer, softer" or "louder, louder, louder" as necessary and appropriate.

Building Blocks

This activity refines speech capacity and promotes the development of spatial concepts.

Most children have difficulty pronouncing certain sounds during early childhood. The tendency to say things like "Thilly wabbit" instead of "Silly rabbit" is quite common and usually temporary.

Natural Varieties

Collect and sort natural objects.

What You'll Need:

outdoor area such as a beach, park, or nature trail

large bucket

Building Blocks

This activity enhances discrimination skills and promotes the development of classification schemes.

Walk through the area with the toddler. As you go, ask her to find a large twig, then a larger one, then a smaller one. Repeat with different items and different adjectives. For example, ask for a large stone, a small one, a rough one, a smooth one, a black one, a white one. As she finds each item, ask her to place them in the bucket. When you return home, pour out the contents of the bucket. Ask the toddler to help you sort everything. Sort the items several times using different sets and subsets. For example, first sort by type of item, then each item of that type by size, color, or texture. Next, sort all of the items by size, color, or texture and then sort the items within each of those groups by type.

Star of the Story

Act out and add on to your favorite stories.

What You'll Need:

favorite story and nursery rhyme books

Building Blocks

This activity stimulates imagination and promotes connections between words and the actions or events they represent.

Read the toddler one of his favorite stories or nursery rhymes. Then read the story again, encouraging him to act out the role of the main character as the action unfolds. Provide any props the toddler may need, and be prepared to act out the roles of other characters yourself. Repeat the game with other stories and nursery rhymes. If he is especially enthusiastic when acting as a particular character, help the toddler create his own "sequel" to the story or rhyme. When the story or rhyme is finished, ask, "What do you think happened next?" and invite the toddler to act out additional scenes. If the toddler is not yet comfortable with supplying the additional plot, provide it yourself and allow him to concentrate on coming up with the corresponding action sequences.

Putting Things in Pairs

Match each object with its mate.

What You'll Need:

collections of paired objects, such as:

shoes, slippers, or boots

gloves or mittens

large pillowcase or laundry bag

Building Blocks

This activity enhances sorting skills and promotes the development of basic number concepts.

Put together several collections of paired items of the same type. Avoid breakable objects or small items, such as earrings that could be swallowed accidentally. Take one pair of each type (one pair of shoes, one pair of empty salt and pepper shakers, one pair of gloves) and put them into the pillowcase or laundry bag. Shake everything up, and then spill them on the floor. Encourage the toddler to pick up items one at a time and then find the matching item. After repeating this several times, increase the challenge. Place all pairs of the same type of item into the pillowcase or laundry bag, shake them up, and spill them out. Invite the toddler to match each shoe, glove, shaker, etc. with its appropriate mate.

An Upside-Down World

It's a new way of seeing!

Stand next to the toddler. Bend over and place your head between your legs. Encourage the toddler to do the same. Talk to him about how things look from that perspective. Keeping your head between your legs, waddle around and invite the toddler to follow along. Continue describing the new sights you encounter as you go. Spend some time in front of a mirror, and invite the toddler to look at the funny faces you make and to make some funny faces himself. Return to a safe open area. Ask the toddler to put his head between his legs again. Hold him securely and help him perform a simple somersault. After he has rolled over several times, grab his ankles and hold him in a headstand position for a few seconds.

Building Blocks

This activity enhances gross motor skills and stimulates the development of spatial concepts.

The inclination of children to say "no" to many parental requests and instructions during the second half of the second year is simply due to their desire to explore and exercise their newly discovered personal power. It is not the expression of a truly negative attitude.

Bring It Here/Put It Back

Collect and return the items on Mom and Dad's lists.

What You'll Need:

pen or marker

index cards

basket or pail

Building Blocks

This activity enhances discrimination and memory skills and stimulates literacy awareness.

Draw pictures of two common household items, such as a slipper and a book, on an index card. Write out the name of the item next to the picture. Give the index card to the toddler, identify the items, and ask her to use the basket or pail to collect the items on the "list." When she has finished collecting them, ask her to put the items back where she found them. Play the game again using different items. Next, create new lists with three items. Use two items from a previous list plus one entirely new one. If the toddler does well with those, try lists with four items. If she has a little trouble replacing the third or fourth items, give her a hint or two.

Parade of Pull Toys

Drag them here and there to produce different sounds.

What You'll Need:

assortment of disposable containers, such as:

cans, milk cartons, shoebox, plastic tubs

screwdriver

string

Make sure that each container you use is unbreakable. Use a screwdriver to punch a hole in the bottom or side of each one. Slide a piece of string through it and tie a large knot at each end to form a pull toy with an easy-to-grasp handle. The string should be long enough for the toddler to hold one end and walk while the item drags along the ground. However, it should be short enough to prevent it from becoming tangled around his legs. Invite the toddler to pull each item along the floor. Talk about the different sounds produced by each one. Encourage the toddler to pull the items along different surfaces within the house, such as carpet, hardwood, tile, and linoleum, and talk about the differences in feel and sound on each surface. Then take the pull toys outside and let him drag them along concrete, gravel, grass, and any other available surfaces.

Building Blocks

This activity enhances sensory discrimination and sorting skills.

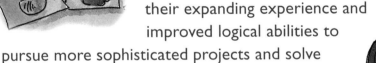

Chapter 6
2-Year-Olds

Between ages 2 and 3, toddlers' imagination and creativity explode. They no longer are content with mere imitation. They put together all sorts of interesting scenarios in their own heads and then act them out enthusiastically with their impressive physical and verbal skills. Their attention span and memory lengthen significantly. During this time, toddlers are fascinated by opportunities to use their expanding experience and improved logical abilities to pursue more sophisticated projects and solve more complicated problems. Their recognition, discrimination, and classification abilities lead them to become increasingly fascinated with concepts relating to letters and numbers. And although parents remain their favorite playmates, their social interest expands to include activities with peers as well.

Dirt Detective

There are amazing things to find in everyday dirt!

What You'll Need:

newspaper

small shovel

dirt

sieve or strainer

magnifying glass

Building Blocks

This activity promotes observation and helps develop categorization skills.

Spread some sheets of newspaper on a table or on the ground outside. Ask the child to dig up a shovelful of dirt and spread it out on the newspaper—or have him strain the dirt through a sieve or strainer. He can search through the dirt, looking for rocks, pebbles, insects, seeds, roots, and other interesting finds. Give him a magnifying glass so he can zero in on the objects and see them better. Then ask the child to sort the underground discoveries into categories. To make the activity more advanced, the child can make a record of his discoveries through drawings.

What Paints How?

Put down your paintbrush and try these unusual painting tools!

What You'll Need:

feather

twigs and leaves

cotton ball

cotton swab

sponge

paint

paper

paintbrush

Here's an artistic way for the child to experiment with a variety of improvised paint tools and have fun noticing the different results that can be achieved using them. Give the child a wide variety of paint tools, including a traditional paintbrush and some nontraditional tools, such as those listed in the box. Let her experiment with the items and draw conclusions about how different tools paint. To make the activity more difficult, include the child when you choose the tools to be used, and continue to add new implements for further testing. To simplify, allow the child to experiment with only two or three very different kinds of implements at a time.

Building Blocks

This activity enhances observation skills and helps develop the ability to make comparisons.

Cooked and Uncooked

Find out whether food tastes different when it's chopped, cooked, or mashed.

What You'll Need:

apples

vegetable peeler

plastic knife

pot

water

potato masher

bowl

spoon

Optional: other vegetables

Building Blocks

This activity develops the child's ability to predict, compare, and observe change.

Prepare one food several different ways and let your child take a taste test. Does cooking change the flavor? Does size or shape make a fruit taste different? Does a shredded vegetable taste the same as an uncut vegetable? The child can make predictions and then test them out. First, make sure everyone washes their hands! Peel and core an apple, then invite the child to help you cut up the apple into small pieces. He can then put the pieces into a pot that contains a small amount of water. Cook the apple slowly, until it is mushy. While the apple is cooking, cut a second apple into slices to be eaten raw. When the cooked apple is soft enough, let the child mash it with a potato masher. Spoon the fresh apple-sauce into a bowl, taste, and compare it to the raw apple slices. Encourage the child to describe the differences, including how each one tastes. To make the activity more difficult, you can also include any of the following in the test: grated apples, uncooked apple-sauce, or fresh apple juice. For uncooked applesauce, put apple slices in a blender and blend with a little bit of water. For a variation on this comparison activity, use carrots. They can be diced, sliced, curled, shredded, cut in sticks, or eaten whole. They can be steamed in chunks or cooked with a little water, then mashed or pureed. They also can be juiced.

Color Coding

This match game can be challenging!

What You'll Need:

paint-sample strips

Give the child a paint-sample strip and ask her to match it to a household item of the same color. Start with the boldest reds, blues, greens, etc., then increase the challenge by providing her with more subtle shades. Point to the written name of the color on the strip and read it for her. Repeat the name as you ask, "Now, can you find something that is colonial blue? Olive green?" If the child is having trouble locating a match, make a game out of supplying hints. For example, say, "I think there might be something in the living room. You're getting warmer, you're getting colder, now you're really hot!" In addition or as an alternative, take the strips along to the beach, the park, or a nature trail. Encourage the child to find matching colors that occur naturally outside.

Puzzle Peeker

Turn pictures into puzzles with a puzzle peeker.

What You'll Need:

paper

scissors

**picture from a book
or magazine**

Make a puzzle peeker by cutting 5 to 8 horizontal strips in a piece of paper to about 1½ inches from the edge. Place the puzzle peeker on top of a picture that your child has not yet seen. Ask her to pull one strip back at a time and try to guess what the picture is. To increase the challenge, place the puzzle peeker on top of a complex picture!

Building Blocks

This activity encourages observation and critical-thinking skills.

By three years of age, children have mastered two-thirds of all the everyday language they will use for the rest of their lives.

Be Still and Smell

With this little nose I smell…?

What You'll Need:

rubber cement

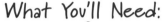

stiff paper squares

variety of spices (such as garlic, cinnamon, oregano)

hole punch

reclosable plastic bags

With your child, make spice cards by spreading rubber cement on a paper square and sprinkling it with a spice. Make two cards for each kind of spice. When the cards have dried, punch several holes in each one so fragrances will waft through for easy smelling when they're facedown. (Be sure the cement has dried before the child smells the cards.) Ask your child to turn all the cards facedown, mix them up, and try to match mates. Encourage him to pick up cards and sniff them, keeping the cards facedown while doing so! For easier sorting, the child can turn over all the cards and use visual cues to help make the matches. Keep the spice cards in self-sealing plastic bags, one kind of spice per bag, when they are not being used.

Building Blocks

This activity helps develop olfactory discrimination.

Weigh Away

Light, lighter, lightest—which is which?

What You'll Need:

hole punch or large nail

two empty plastic tubs of equal size

yarn

scissors

hanger

assorted items, such as stuffed animals, toy cars, blocks

Let your child help you make a simple balance scale. First, punch or poke three holes equidistantly around the rim of the two plastic margarine tubs. Cut six pieces of yarn all the same size. Thread a piece of yarn though a hole and tie one end of it to the tub; repeat for all holes and all pieces of yarn. Then tie the three strings of one tub on one end of a hanger and the three strings from the other tub on the other end. Now you have a balance scale! Hang the scale on a door-knob. Once the scale is set up, encourage the child to gather an assortment of items, predict which will be heavier or lighter, and then test those predictions by putting the items in the scale. To make the activity more challenging, the child can continue to compare a group of objects until she is able to put them in order from lightest to heaviest. She can also make predictions about how many of a lighter object it will take to equal the weight of a heavier one.

Building Blocks

This activity helps develop predicting, testing, comparing, and ordering skills.

Scavenger Hunt

Can you find what's on your list?

What You'll Need:

check-off list

clipboard or cardboard and large paper clip

pencil

old magazines

nontoxic white glue

yarn

Children are naturally observant of their surroundings, so go on a scavenger hunt and make a game out of it. Create a list of things to look for. The list can be made of pictures, either line drawings or pictures cut from magazines and glued to the list, or it can be words for young readers. Items pictured might include a dog, bird, mailbox, stop sign, something orange, and something yellow. Tie a pencil to a clipboard with yarn, and invite the child to carry the list as you take a walk through the neighborhood. Let him check off each item he discovers.

Building Blocks

This activity helps refine observation skills and encourages the development of reading skills.

Snack Face at My Place

Smile at a snack that will smile back!

What You'll Need:

plate

plastic knife

peanut butter or cream cheese

rice cakes

toppings (olives, carrot slices, apple slices, raisins, walnut halves)

First, have everyone wash their hands. Put a plate, a plastic knife, and the food items listed in the box on a table and invite the child to make faces out of them. Have her start by spreading peanut butter or cream cheese on a rice cake (or any round cracker or bread). Mouths, noses, and eyes (and ears and eyebrows and mustaches, if desired!) can be created by placing assorted toppings on the spread. The child can tell you about the face snack and then eat it as a treat. To make the activity more unusual and intriguing, invite the child to create three or four different faces. Then carefully cut each of the faces in half. The child can mix and match the faces before eating them!

Building Blocks

This activity encourages creative thinking.

Imaginary Snow

Create clouds and snow with silky, fluffy, puffy white foam!

What You'll Need:

plastic tablecloth

shaving cream

waterproof smock

plastic animals or cars

Spread a plastic tablecloth over a table and spray it with mounds of shaving cream. Put a smock on the child, and invite him to mold and mush and slosh the foamy cream, enjoying and talking about the texture. (Remind the child not to rub his eyes with foamy fingers.) The child can form the foam into puffy clouds, snowy mountains, or imaginary white worlds or have fun making patterns and designs in it. Plastic animals, cars, and other toys can be used for active story-making. On a warm summer day, this activity can be done outside in a bathing suit!

Building Blocks

This activity promotes tactile experiences and storytelling skills.

Look, Listen, and Do

Play a clapping, snapping, stomping, jumping pattern game!

Make up two-part patterns using clapping, patting, or other body movements. Demonstrate a pattern, such as clap-stomp-clap-stomp-clap-stomp, and then invite the child to repeat the pattern. As she gains more experience, she can try a hand (or foot!) at making up her own two-part patterns. Take turns making up patterns for one another to repeat and continue. Increase the challenge by including some three-part patterns in the game. For an even greater challenge, take turns adding an action to one another's pattern. For example, the adult might make up the pattern: clap-tap. The child can repeat it, and then change it by turning it into the three-part pattern: clap-tap-stomp. The adult can repeat it and then add one more: clap-tap-stomp-wiggle.

Building Blocks

This activity helps develop recognition, repetition, and patterning skills.

Marshmallow Minaret

Build towers and castles with easy-to-use (and eat!) materials.

What You'll Need:

miniature marshmallows

toothpicks

peanut butter

plastic knife

Invite the child to build structures with miniature marshmallows, using the toothpicks to hold joints together. He can make any type of structure, including towers or castles, people, creatures, or abstract objects. For a variation, combine large and small marshmallows, use white or colored marshmallows, or use peanut butter instead of toothpicks for glue!

Building Blocks

This activity promotes creative thinking, planning, and problem-solving skills.

Can You See My Face?

Turn twigs and leaves and odds and ends into found faces!

What You'll Need:

assorted household and nature objects, such as:

bottle caps

buttons

rubber bands

twigs and leaves

paper

Building Blocks

This activity helps develop problem-solving skills and creative and symbolic thinking.

Gather assorted natural and household items. Challenge the child to arrange items on a piece of paper to create a face. To make it easier to begin, suggest that she start by picking an item to use for a nose, and then ask her where to place it on the paper. If the child has difficulty, have her look at the shape and position of your nose. After that, it's a simple matter of picking eyes and a mouth. Other features can also be added. After a face is finished, take turns making changes by replacing parts of the face with different items.

Spoon a Ping-Pong Along

Try a tricky athletic feat with just a Ping-Pong ball and a spoon!

What You'll Need:

Ping-Pong ball

serving spoon

Building Blocks

This activity helps develop gross-motor and problem-solving skills.

Challenge the child to carry a Ping-Pong ball in a serving spoon across a room without dropping it. This is not easy to do and may take some practice! After the child has mastered the task, make it even trickier. How fast can he carry the ball across the room without dropping it? Can he carry it while weaving around several chairs instead of straight across the room? Create a simple obstacle course with the child to test his Ping-Pong-ball-carrying skill!

Mood Match

What makes people happy? What makes them sad?
Try to make a match.

What You'll Need:

pictures of people with different facial expressions and pictures of places, things, or activities cut from magazines

Gather an assortment of pictures cut from magazines of people expressing a variety of emotions. Gather an equal number of pictures of places, events, and things. Invite the child to match the happy, sad, frightened, or angry people with pictures that show something that might have caused the person to feel that way. Encourage her to explain why she made the choices she did.

Building Blocks

This activity helps develop categorization, matching, and interpretation skills.

Achieving a Balance

There's no fear of falling from this home balance beam!

What You'll Need:

masking tapes of different widths

Building Blocks

This activity refines body control and motor skills and helps build self-confidence.

Place a long strip (at least 10 feet) of wide masking tape on the ground or floor. Demonstrate walking along the tape, making sure your feet do not touch the ground or floor on either side of the tape. Invite the child to walk along the tape strip as well. Once he is comfortable crossing this "balance beam" without "falling off," increase the challenge. Place a long strip of masking tape that is a little less wide on the ground or floor and ask him to try again. Keep using progressively narrower strips of masking tape. Then go back to the widest strip of masking tape and encourage the child to try running the entire length. Increase the running challenge by using progressively narrower strips of masking tape.

Yarn Cylinders

*'Round and 'round and 'round you go, making
a variety of brightly decorated containers.*

What You'll Need:

**cylindrical containers of
various sizes**

double-sided tape

**yarns of
different colors**

Collect an assortment of clean, empty, unbreakable cylindrical containers (oatmeal boxes, plastic juice bottles, salt boxes). Wrap each one from top to bottom with double-sided tape. Cut many colors of yarn into strips of different lengths. Show the child how to decorate the container by sticking the yarn to the tape. Start by wrapping yarn completely around the container horizontally. Next, go vertically, from top to bottom. Then place strips of yarn at interesting angles. Ask the child to decorate the other cylinders. In addition, invite her to make a special project out of the largest container. Tell her to start at the bottom and make one complete circle with blue yarn, then two complete circles with red yarn, three with green, and so on until she reaches the top. Help her count the total number of circles she has made when she is finished.

Stack and Crush

Jump into the fun of preparing boxes for recycling!

What You'll Need:

large assortment of empty cardboard grocery boxes

Take a box and demonstrate how to crush it by jumping on it. Invite the child to do the same with various boxes. Then encourage him to make piles of two or three boxes and crush them all at once. When all the boxes are crushed, ask the child to help you sort them by size. Together, make one big pile, placing the largest boxes on the bottom and the smallest on top. Let him knock over and rebuild the pile as often as he likes. When he is done playing with the boxes, ask him to help you put them in an appropriate container. Take the child with you to a recycling bin or center, and explain to him the benefits of being environmentally responsible.

Building Blocks

This activity enhances gross-motor skills and promotes social awareness.

Personal Stenographer

Take turns telling about and recording recent events.

What You'll Need:

notepad and pen

Building Blocks

This activity stimulates recall capacity and promotes the development of connections between verbal and written communication.

After a trip to the park, zoo, or supermarket; after an event such as a birthday party or holiday celebration; or after a visit to a relative's house, ask the child to tell you all about what happened. As she does, write down everything she says. If she leaves out certain episodes and details, prompt her. When the child is done reporting, show her what you've written and read it back to her. Encourage her to tell you all about other things as well. Ask her to describe the contents of her room or to talk about various family members. Record and then read these accounts, too. If the child is interested in playing the role of the stenographer, give her a pad of paper and a crayon. Tell her about something yourself, and let her scribble away as you talk.

Itty Bitty Teeny Tiny Me

Pretend to be teeny tiny for a little itty bit of fun!

Ask the child to make believe that he is very, very small and to do everything in an itty bitty teeny tiny way. Here are some possibilities: Take itty bitty teeny tiny steps when walking. Take itty bitty teeny tiny bites of food when eating. Make an itty bitty teeny tiny drawing on a teeny tiny itty bitty piece of paper. Encourage the child to think of many different actions and activities to try out in a small way. Later on, the child can try doing everything in a GREAT BIG GIANT WAY!

Building Blocks

This activity encourages creative-thinking and problem-solving skills.

Toddlers are often inclined to use "telegraphic" speech, leaving out words that are not essential (as people used to do when sending telegrams). For example, it is not uncommon for them to abbreviate simple sentences, saying, "What doing?" instead of "What are you doing?"

Chapter 7
3-Year-Olds

During the third year, children become much more active in their own education. Their interests expand far beyond their own home and family. They use their greatly improved mental capacities to absorb, organize, and store as much information as they can from the objects and events that fascinate them. They also use their imagination and creativity to experiment with ideas as well as things. Three-year-olds become acutely aware of the "rules" of language, social interactions, daily routines, and the way things work. And although their interpretation of the rules may be overly rigid at times, this new understanding enables them to make significant progress in laying the groundwork for reading, writing, and arithmetic.

Walking Ways

Traipse and tramp to tell a tale!

Invite the child to act out walking in a variety of manners to communicate different ideas. Together with the child, think up a variety of situations and take turns acting them out. Here are some examples to start with:

• Walk as if it's pouring rain.

• Walk as if you're in a great hurry.

• Walk as if you can't wait to get to the park.

• Walk as if you don't want to go somewhere.

• Walk as if you are being followed by a bear.

• Walk as if you're on the moon.

To make the activity simpler, invite the child to walk across the room the way a cat, dog, mouse, duck, or elephant might.

Building Blocks
This activity develops interpretive skills and the use of the body to communicate ideas.

Body Parts Mix-Up

Mix and match to make unusual creatures and critters.

What You'll Need:

magazine pictures of people and animals

scissors

paper

nontoxic white glue

Cut out pictures of people and animals from old magazines. Then cut the pictures further to create an assortment of heads, legs, wings, arms, torsos, and tails. Ask the child to reassemble the body parts to make new creatures and then glue them together on a sheet of paper. He can then talk about or describe what he has invented, or he can make up stories about these new creatures!

Building Blocks

This activity helps develop the concept of parts and whole as well as creative-thinking skills.

Three Things Stories

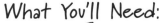

Put people, places, and things together in new and unusual ways!

What You'll Need:

pictures of people, places, and things cut from magazines

nontoxic white glue

white paper

paper bags

marker

Gather an assortment of pictures of people, places, and things cut from magazines. Mount the pictures on white paper. Include as wide a variety of subjects as possible. After all the pictures are cut, mounted, and gathered, invite the child to sort the pictures into three piles: one for people, one for places, and one for things. Take 3 paper bags and label one for people, one for places, and one for things. Open the bags and stand them up in a row. When the pictures have been sorted, place each of the piles into the appropriate paper bag. Take turns choosing one picture from each category and telling ways the three pictures go together. The reasons can be realistic or entirely fanciful! To encourage fantasy, you can start the game giving examples of how the first three things might go together in a story. After the storyteller has explained the ways the pictures go together, the listener can ask three questions of the teller to elicit more details. To simplify the game, use only two categories: people and places or people and things.

Building Blocks

This activity encourages creative-thinking, critical-thinking, and language skills.

Sounding Off

Make lots of noise—all with your parent's approval!

What You'll Need:

variety of containers with tops, such as coffee can, film canister, margarine tub, oatmeal box

fillers, such as uncooked rice or kidney beans, paper clips and buttons

Building Blocks

This activity enhances auditory discrimination.

Exploring noise-making is natural for a young child, but listening takes practice and skill! Let the child experiment with sounds by putting different amounts and kinds of materials into a variety of containers and then closing them, shaking them, and listening. To simplify the activity, decrease the variables: The child can use containers that are all the same size and shape but fill them with different materials. Or, he can fill containers of different sizes and shapes with varying amounts of the same material. To increase the difficulty, ask the child to line up the containers in order from the softest noisemaker to the loudest. (Supervise young children; small objects can be choking hazards.)

Beautiful Beads

Transform everyday items into decorative beads!

What You'll Need:

measuring cup

flour

salt

cornstarch

bowl

water

unsharpened pencil or chenille stem

paintbrush and paint

yarn

Have the child help measure ¾ cup flour, ½ cup salt, and ½ cup cornstarch into a bowl. Add water to form a dough. Take turns kneading the dough. When the dough is pliable, show the child how to form beads by rolling round little handfuls of the dough into balls. The child can make holes in the beads with the end of a pencil or chenille stem. Set the beads out to dry. After they have dried, she can paint them. When the paint is dry, the child can string the beads on yarn for wearing or for decoration! For a decoration variation, tie several strands of beads to a dowel with yarn for a pretty mobile.

Building Blocks

This activity helps children learn to follow steps in a process and enhances measuring and observational abilities.

Story Cards

Use magazine pictures to elicit entertaining tales!

What You'll Need:

magazines

scissors

paper

nontoxic white glue

Encourage the child to choose pictures of assorted subjects, such as people, animals, places, foods, shoes, etc., from magazines. Have him cut out 10 to 12 of the pictures. Glue each picture onto a separate piece of paper to create the story cards. When the glue is dry, turn the papers facedown and spread them out. Ask the child to turn over three of the story cards and make up a story that includes all three pictures. You can also use the story cards for cooperative storytelling. One person chooses a card from the facedown cards and begins a story about that picture. The next person chooses another card and makes up the next part of the story, incorporating that picture. Keep going until there are no more cards or you're tired of the story.

Building Blocks

This activity promotes the development of creative-thinking, sequencing, and problem-solving skills.

How Big Around?

Here's another way to measure size.

What You'll Need:

yarn

scissors

apple, carrot, pumpkin, radish, watermelon, or other fruits and vegetables

It's common to measure how short, tall, long, or wide something is, but not how big around! Measuring the circumference of various fruits and vegetables can lead to surprising results when the round distances are spread out into flat lengths and compared to one another. Give the child some yarn to use for measuring. You can precut the yarn into separate pieces to make the measuring easier. Ask the child to measure around each fruit or vegetable with the yarn and then cut the yarn to that size. She can then line up the strips and compare them.

Building Blocks

This activity encourages the development of prediction and comparison skills and provides experience with measuring.

Danger! Volcano Eruption!

Create bubbling, fizzy explosions for dramatic science play.

What You'll Need:

sand or dirt

empty can

vinegar

food coloring

baking soda

Optional: water, milk, lemonade

Building Blocks

This activity helps develop observational skills and encourages experimentation.

With the child, make a volcanic mountain out of sand or dirt that's in a sandbox, a large box, or an outside play area. Help him place an empty can, open end up, in the top of the mountain. The child can then fill the can halfway with vinegar and add a few drops of food coloring. Then have him add a spoonful of baking soda. Watch the eruption! Talk with the child about chemical reactions and explain that when baking soda is mixed with an acid it causes a reaction (creating the carbon dioxide "explosion"). The child might want to experiment further (with adult supervision) to discover other liquids that will have the same effect when mixed with baking soda. The child can try putting a spoonful of baking soda into $\frac{1}{2}$ cup each of water, milk, and lemonade to see what the results are.

Melt-and-Eat Collages

Create edible artwork that transforms in the oven!

What You'll Need:

knife

butter

bread

cookie sheet and a broiler

cheese slices

sliced cold cuts

scissors

chopped tomato

Butter the bread and place it buttered-side down on the cookie sheet. Invite the child to use the scissors to cut out different shapes from the cheese and cold cuts. After she has produced a collection of shapes, encourage her to use the pieces of cheese and cold cuts along with the tomato bits to create a "collage" on the bread. She can make a face, a building, or simply an abstract work of art. Butter additional pieces of bread and let her produce more creations. Place the creations in the broiler until the cheese melts. Remove the cookie sheet and let the child observe the results. Make sure she doesn't touch the cookie sheet or the food while it is hot. When the food has cooled sufficiently, put her creations on a plate and let her eat them.

Building Blocks

This activity refines fine motor skills, stimulates imagination, and teaches basic science concepts.

I Did Spy

Play a variation of the traditional "I Spy" game.

This game can be played indoors or out. Taking turns, one person starts by taking a look all around and then closing his eyes. The second person, with eyes open, asks questions about things in the room that the first person tries to answer while keeping his eyes closed. The questions are quick-take observation questions, such as: Is your blue sweater on the bed or the chair? How many books are on the table? What color is the towel that's hanging on the line?

Building Blocks

This activity develops observation and critical-thinking skills.

Author! Author!

Add to a private library by making a personal book!

What You'll Need:

construction paper

scissors

hole punch

chenille stems

markers

Building Blocks

This activity promotes the expression of ideas and develops reading-related skills.

Cut construction paper into equal-sized squares. Ask the child to count out 5 sheets of paper and punch a hole in the corner of each of the squares. Then the child can loop a chenille stem through the holes and twist the ends. She can draw a story in the book and share it. Make blank books ahead of time for just the right moment—when the author is ready to write or draw! Another way to fasten the books is to punch several holes along one edge and weave a chenille stem through the holes.

Vocabulary Dance

Learn new action words to create a dance!

What You'll Need:

CD or tape player

favorite CDs or tapes

Building Blocks

This activity refines large muscle skills and enhances language acquisition.

Play a favorite tune. Ask the child to join you as you create a special dance to go along with the song. Start with simple movements and instructions, such as "run" and "jump." Gradually make the dance more complicated by adding new words, such as "leap," "twirl," and "stretch." Make sure to model the appropriate movements that go along with the new words. After the child has become comfortable with a variety of movements, add directional cues as well. For example, say, "Run forward, jump back, twirl around this way, twirl around the other way, leap to this side, leap to that side." If the child indicates an inclination to take the lead, follow his movements and describe what he is doing.

leap

How Many Will Fit?

1, 2, 3—How many can there be?

What You'll Need:

small clear plastic jar

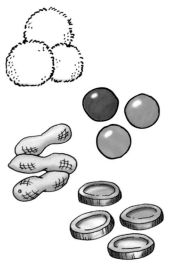

collection of the same kind of items, such as cotton balls, marbles, peanuts, and poker chips

Building Blocks

This activity enhances estimating and number skills.

It's traditional to look at a group of items and estimate how many there are. Here's a backward way to estimate! Ask the child to look at a small container and a group of objects and estimate how many of the objects will fit inside the container! The child can then check the estimation by counting the objects while placing them inside. For easy estimating, use a small clear jar and objects large enough so that only 5 to 10 will fit inside. To increase the difficulty use larger jars and smaller items!

It Sounds Like This!

Use your imagination and skill to imitate natural sounds.

Challenge the child to listen to the sounds all around and to invent sounds to imitate them. The child might try to imitate natural sounds, such as wind, rain, or thunder, or household sounds, such as running water or the broom when a parent sweeps the floor. For more of a challenge, play a sound-guessing game. Take turns imitating nature and household sounds for the other person to guess.

Building Blocks

This activity helps develop critical-thinking and listening skills.

When two languages are spoken in the home, children initially are a little slow to reach the standard language development milestones in each language. But by 3 or 4 years of age, they usually are fluent in both languages.

boom

What's Missing?

How good is your memory?

What You'll Need:

common household objects such as:

sock

teddy bear

postage stamp

playing card

ballpoint pen

Play this detective game together to work on observation skills. Take turns being the hider and the detective. The hider chooses 5 items (such as a fork, sock, teddy bear, pencil, key chain) to display on a table for the detective to observe. The detective takes a good look, then covers her eyes. The hider removes one of the objects and hides it out of view! After the object is hidden, the detective uncovers her eyes and takes a second look to figure out what the missing item is. To increase the challenge, add more items to the table.

Building Blocks

This activity promotes observation skills and helps develop memory.

Water Melodies

Be the composer of your own "water music"!

What You'll Need:

glasses and glass jars

plastic tub

water pitcher and water

spoon

Building Blocks

This activity fine-tunes auditory discrimination.

Here's a simple way to create pretty sounds. Help the child place glasses and glass jars in a plastic tub and fill them with different amounts of water. The child can then gently tap the glasses with a spoon to make sounds. The sound of each jar or glass can be modified either by adding more water from the water pitcher or by removing some water from the tub. Encourage the child to explore altering the sound of each "instrument" as well as creating his own tunes. To make this more difficult, ask the child to place the glasses in order from the highest pitch to the lowest, according to the sound scale. If the glasses are different sizes and shapes, the child will need to rely fully on listening skills in order to complete this task. To simplify, use fewer glasses that are all of the same size and shape. For an added challenge, ask the child to figure out how much water to add to two differently shaped glasses in order to get the same sound when each one is tapped.

Invisible Painting

Watercolors reveal the invisible drawing.

What You'll Need:

white wax candle

white paper

watercolor paints

paintbrush

dark marker pen

Use the candle to draw a pattern or scene on a sheet of paper. The wax drawing will be almost invisible. Ask the child to paint the entire sheet with watercolor paints. As the paint dries, the pattern or scene will appear. Encourage the child to draw or simply scribble on other sheets of paper with the candle. Then let her paint those sheets and reveal her invisible creations. On other sheets, use the dark marker pen to write out the names of simple objects, such as "apple," "bottle," or "cat." Then use the candle to draw a picture of the object. Encourage the child to use her "detective" skills to find the invisible object that goes with the word you've written on each sheet.

Building Blocks

This activity stimulates imagination and promotes basic literacy skills.

Vehicle Tally

Keep track of cars and trucks with a graph and tally!

What You'll Need:

tally sheet

clipboard

pencil

Building Blocks

This activity develops sorting, counting, and graphing skills.

Divide the tally sheet into 3 to 5 columns labeled with simple pictures of common vehicles, and attach it to a clipboard. Take the clipboard and pencil with you to a park or the sidewalk near your house—somewhere it is easy to watch cars driving by. Ask the child to predict what kind of vehicle will pass by most often. Label each of the columns (pictures are best). The child can choose the column categories. The child might choose vehicle types (truck, car, motorcycle, van) or car colors (yellow cars, blue cars, red cars). Write down predictions of which vehicles the child expects to see most and which he expects to see least. Then let him keep track of the sightings by tallying the passing cars in the correct columns. When one of the columns is all checked off, stop the tally and check against the predictions.

For a further challenge, take the same tally at different times of the day or on different days, and compare all the tallies to see if the results are the same or different.

Legendary Lists

Invent fanciful categories and fill them with imaginary listings.

Take turns creating categories and challenging one another to name real or pretend events, ideas, or items that fit into them. Encourage the child to have fun and be creative when making the list! Some examples of categories that you might suggest for one another are: important items to take along on a trip to Mars; new holidays that should be invented; unusual ways to use a paper cup; new flavors of ice cream that might be created. For further fun, turn a fanciful list into a fiction story!

Building Blocks

This activity promotes the development of critical-thinking and creative-thinking skills.

Solve the Problem

Step into a story and be a problem solver.

What You'll Need:

**favorite story
or book**

Building Blocks

This activity develops problem-solving and creative-thinking skills.

Read a book together, but stop the story at the height of a problem. Then ask the child to describe what he might do in a similar situation. Encourage him to give reasons and explain his choices.

Chapter 8
4-Year-Olds

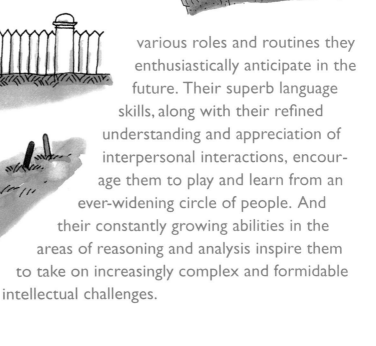

Four-year-olds are actively preparing to become full-fledged students and citizens. They eagerly pursue and absorb experiences that feed their insatiable curiosity about the subtleties and complexities of their environment. Their vastly improved attention span and memory capacity enable them to accurately relate current activities to past experiences, and their imagination and creativity permit them to "practice" various roles and routines they enthusiastically anticipate in the future. Their superb language skills, along with their refined understanding and appreciation of interpersonal interactions, encourage them to play and learn from an ever-widening circle of people. And their constantly growing abilities in the areas of reasoning and analysis inspire them to take on increasingly complex and formidable intellectual challenges.

What Would You Do?

Share the solution with a display of dramatic action!

Take turns making up imaginary situations, and challenge one another to act out what one might do. These are some possible situations to get you started:

• What would you do if 5 lions walked in the kitchen while you were eating lunch?

• What would you do if you woke up in the morning and discovered you'd been sleeping in a tree?

• What would you do if the cat came to the kitchen table and asked for breakfast cereal?

Building Blocks

This activity develops problem-solving skills.

What's Dot?

Start with one dot to create a whole picture!

What You'll Need:

stick-on dots

paper

crayons

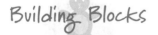

scissors

Place one stick-on dot anywhere on a piece of paper. Let the child decide what the dot will become and draw the rest of the picture around the dot. (The dot could be an animal head, the tip of someone's hat, a ball that children are throwing, etc.) If he enjoys this activity, on another day give him a paper with a small hole in it as a picture challenge. Cut out a hole approximately 1 inch in diameter anywhere on the paper—or have the child tell you how big to cut the hole and where. Invite him to draw a picture around the hole, incorporating the hole into the picture any way he likes. (For instance, it might be a hole a worker is digging, the open mouth of a bear, the moon, or part of a design.)

Building Blocks

This activity develops problem-solving and creative-thinking skills.

Building Together Apart

It's a challenge to build the same building as someone else without looking!

What You'll Need:

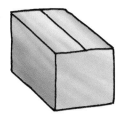

large cardboard box

scissors

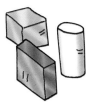

set of blocks

Create a divider by cutting off the flaps on both ends of a large cardboard box and then cutting along the fold of 2 panels. Set the divider up on a table or on the floor. Divide a set of blocks so that each person (an adult and a child or 2 children) has the identical number, size, and shape of blocks. Position one person on one side of the divider and the other on the other side, making sure that neither can see what the other person is doing. One person builds a building, describing each step of the building process: what kind of block is being used and where it is being placed. The other person tries to make the same building at the same time by listening to and following the directions. When the 2 buildings are finished, remove the divider and compare the buildings. Then take down the buildings, put the divider back up, and reverse the roles!

Building Blocks

This activity develops speaking, listening, and critical-thinking skills.

Which One Doesn't Go?

Use logic to figure out what doesn't belong.

What You'll Need:

pictures cut from magazines

Provide the child with groups of 4 pictures in which one thing doesn't belong. For example, give her pictures of ice cream, donuts, cookies, and broccoli or pictures of sneakers, rain boots, ballet shoes, and an umbrella. Challenge the child to figure out which item doesn't belong and explain why. For further play, encourage the child to suggest a fourth item that *would* go with the group!

Building Blocks

This activity develops critical-thinking and classification skills.

Finding the "In Group"

Create categories, then figure out what fits in and what doesn't.

What You'll Need:

2 long lengths of yarn or string

household objects such as:

paper clips

bottle caps

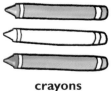

crayons

buttons

Building Blocks

This activity helps develop the math concepts of inclusion and exclusion.

Make 2 large circles using the 2 lengths of yarn or string, and have the circles overlap so there is a middle section. This is called a Venn diagram. Explain to the child that you can use the three sections for creating categories. Discuss together the idea of categories and that each circle of yarn will contain a category of items, while the section where the yarn circles overlap will be used for any items that fit in both categories. Use some of the collected objects as an example (beware of a choking hazard with small items). One circle might be for buttons. Place all the buttons from the assorted objects into that circle. The other circle might be for blue things. The child can find all the blue things and place those in the second circle. That might include a blue crayon, a blue plastic animal, and a blue bottle cap. Ask the child if there are any items that are both buttons and blue. Explain that those items fit in both categories, so they go in the middle section. Remove all the items from the 2 circles and intersecting section and place them back in the group of assorted items. Invite the child to come up with 2 new categories for the items and to create a new Venn diagram. You can also sort pictures into the 2 circles.

Hey! A Survey!

Take a tally of friends, neighbors, and family.

What You'll Need:

paper

pencil

clipboard or cardboard and large paper clip

string or yarn

Building Blocks

This activity develops graphing, recording, and data-interpretation skills.

For a simple survey, create a check-off tally sheet with 2 columns. Decide with the child whether he wants to ask a yes/no question (Do you like chocolate ice cream?) or a two-choice question (What do you like better, dogs or cats?). If he's decided to ask a yes/no question, label the top of one row "Yes" and the other "No." For a two-choice question, label the top of each row with one of the choices. Clip the tally sheet on a clipboard or to a piece of cardboard with a paper clip. Tie the pencil onto the clipboard with yarn so the child won't be walking around holding the pencil. The child can then survey family members, friends, and neighbors and record the results on the sheet. When he's finished with his survey, count up the rows together and see what the results are. For more of a challenge, help the child come up with a community-issue question for a neighborhood survey, such as "Do you think we need a stop sign at the corner?" or "Do you think dogs should always be on leashes?" Create a tally form and accompany the child to survey the neighbors!

Puppet Problems

Help perplexed puppets with their problems!

What You'll Need:

markers

paper lunch bags

scissors

felt or paper scraps

nontoxic white glue

crumpled newspaper

paper towel tubes

yarn

Make some simple puppets together by drawing faces on a paper lunch bag with markers. (Or, cut out shapes from felt or paper scraps for the face and glue them on the bag.) Stuff the bag with crumpled newspaper, and insert a paper towel tube in the bottom of the bag. Scrunch the end of the bag around the tube, and secure it by tying a piece of yarn around it. Use the tube as a handle for the puppet. When the puppets are finished, pose a problem that the 2 puppets might be having for the child to help solve. Either the adult can speak for the puppets and the child can act as an intermediary or the adult can use 1 puppet and the child the other, and the 2 puppets can talk to each other to work out the dispute. To make the activity easy, present problems that are not interpersonal; for example, one of the puppets might have trouble finding a lost toy or be afraid of sleeping with the light turned off—so it needs advice!

Building Blocks

This activity promotes critical-thinking and language skills.

Say It Another Way

Find new words to say the same thing.

Take turns making statements and challenging one another to say the same thing in another way. For example, "I went to the park to play—I skipped to the grassy place to have fun" or "The dog is hungry—Our pet wants food." To simplify, invite the child to replace one descriptive word with another. For example, ask the child to find another word to explain that a cookie tastes good (yummy, delicious, great) or that it would be fun (neat, great, exciting) to go to the park.

Building Blocks

This activity promotes critical-thinking and language skills.

Having an imaginary friend is common and normal. It usually indicates a rich imagination and a fondness for pretend play rather than some sort of socialization problem.

Acting Out Musical Stories

Listen and retell a story using music and action, not words!

What You'll Need:

instrumental music that tells a story, such as *Peter and the Wolf* or *The Nutcracker Suite*

tape recorder or CD player

Share a recording of story-based instrumental music with the child. Talk briefly about the story before listening to the music. Then listen together, sharing reactions to the story portrayal. Listen a second time, inviting the child to act out the story to the music. For a variation, invite him to listen to instrumental music that doesn't illustrate any specific story. Let the child invent his own story and act it out in movement to the music.

Guesstimating At Home

Turn everyday experiences into estimating opportunities!

Challenge the child to make guesstimates (estimating guesses) around the home. She can make a prediction and then test it out. For example, ask the child to guesstimate how many steps it is from the bed to the closet, how many boxes of cereal are on the shelf, or how many toothbrushes are in the bathroom. Then go with the child to check the guesstimates!

Building Blocks

This activity promotes the development of estimating and counting skills.

Hidden-camera studies have revealed that although "sibling rivalry" behaviors may be extremely intense when the parents are present, siblings tend to be far more friendly and play well together when they are alone with each other.

Accumulating Memories

Share observations by creating a cooperative cumulative list!

After a trip to the market, a visit to the park, or just a backyard adventure, have one person report one thing he observed. The other person then repeats the first observation and adds another. For example: We saw a caterpillar; We saw a caterpillar and a worm; We saw a caterpillar and a worm and the blue sky. Keep taking turns and adding observations, and see how long a list you each can remember and repeat! When the list gets too long, start another one with observations about a different adventure, and see how long that list can get! To play another version of this game, take turns naming 3 things you each observed. Then take turns seeing how many of the 6 things named each person can remember!

Building Blocks

This activity promotes memory, listening, and language skills.

Once Upon a Prop

Spark cooperative tale-telling with a bagful of commonplace props

What You'll Need:

large bag or pillowcase filled with 6 to 10 common items such as:

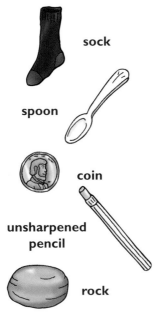

sock

spoon

coin

unsharpened pencil

rock

Fill a bag or pillowcase with a small assortment of commonplace items. The child can help choose the items. When the story bag is ready, reach into the bag and, without looking, choose one of the items. Begin a story using the prop as part of the plot! Then invite the child to take a turn, asking her to close her eyes, pick a prop, and make up the next part of the story, weaving the prop into it. Continue taking turns picking a prop and adding it to the story until the last prop is chosen, signaling time to make up the story ending (which includes the last prop, of course).

Building Blocks

This activity develops problem-solving, creative-thinking, and language skills.

Word Search

Track down and recognize words all around!

When you are walking around the house or the neighborhood, challenge the child to find words that he can read. These might be words that the child can sound out and read or words that he recognizes (such as Cheerios or STOP). As a variation, the child can start a collection of pictures and labels of recognizable words. The saved words can be kept in a box or used for a word collage. You can also start a "Word Wall," where you list all the words the child can read. As the list grows, the child will feel great accomplish- ment!

Building Blocks

This activity develops word recognition and emergent reading skills.

Taking It to the Bank

Loose change turns into a money-sorting game.

What You'll Need:

empty plastic tubs with lids

scissors

index cards

marker

tape

collection of loose change

Cut a slit in the top of each lid. Write 1¢: penny, 5¢: nickel, 10¢: dime, and 25¢: quarter on the different index cards, and tape one to each tub. Pour out the loose change in front of the tubs and show the child which coins go into each tub. Ask her to sort the remainder of the change, and help her count how many of each kind of coin there are in the piles. Then ask the child to "take the money to the bank" by placing the coins in the appropriate tubs. Keep the tubs in an area to which she has easy access. Any time you have collected a pile of spare change, give the child the coins and let her repeat the exercise. Open the tubs occasionally to make sure the contents are consistent.

Building Blocks

This activity promotes counting and classification skills, and it stimulates awareness of practical math applications.

What Does It Mean?

*Listen, then listen **again** to find a word's meaning.*

Choose a word or word phrase that the child is not familiar with for this sleuthing game. Tell him the word, but do not explain what it means. Then use the word in a sentence that gives a clue to the meaning of the word. Continue to make up new sentences using the word in different ways until the child is able to figure out what it means! Start off with easy words or word phrases (for example, supper, stocking). Increase the difficulty by using less concrete words, such as "lazy," whose meaning can be guessed from the context.

Building Blocks

This activity develops critical-thinking and listening skills.

During this year, coordination and balance improves, allowing children to become more independent in self-care tasks such as getting dressed, brushing their teeth, and combing or brushing their hair.

Olympic Distances

This event challenges you to beat your own record!

What You'll Need:

popsicle sticks

Frisbee

tennis ball

wiffle ball

marble

Pick a spot in the yard or park from which the child can safely throw the various objects. Mark the popsicle sticks with different colors to represent each object she'll be throwing. Ask the child to throw each one as far as she can, and use the popsicle sticks to indicate how far each one traveled. Encourage the child to note the distance and then retrieve all of the objects. Challenge her to beat her "record" by throwing each object again. Talk to her about the different objects and why some are easier or more difficult to throw long distances. Return to the yard or park from time to time for additional attempts. Make sure to cheer and applaud the child whenever she succeeds in breaking one of her old records.

Building Blocks

This activity enhances gross-motor abilities, self-esteem, and classification skills.

Can You Tipplefizzy Me?

Play a word-detective game.

One person chooses a common word (water, cat, shoes), keeping it a secret. Then he makes up a sentence using "tipplefizzy" to substitute for the secret word. (I'm thirsty, I want a glass of tipplefizzy.) Use tipplefizzy in as many different sentences as possible until the other person can guess what word tipplefizzy is being used for!

Building Blocks

This activity helps develop listening and critical-thinking skills.

A 4-year-old's vocabulary includes an average of 1,500 words, and that number will increase to 2,500 by his fifth birthday.

What's the Opposite?

Play a contradictory challenge game!

Take turns changing each other's words and statements into their opposites! Start off with easy words to think of opposites for, such as hot (cold), rainy (sunny), happy (sad). Then try to turn simple sentences around! For example: A little girl ran home./A big boy walked to the store.

Building Blocks

This activity promotes the development of critical-thinking and language skills.

There is no "best" method for teaching children to read. Some children learn better with a phonics system while other children learn better with a "whole language" approach. Most, however, learn better with a combination of the two.

Sequel Stories

Imagine what happens after the story ends!

Encourage the child to think about what happens after a favorite story ends. What do the people and animals do next? Do they have any other problems? Adventures? Funny experiences? Do they stay in the same place, move far away, or go on a vacation? Do they meet any new people? After reading or retelling a favorite story, invite the child to make up and tell a story about what happens after the story ends! For a variation, ask the child to imagine and tell what took place just before the story began.

Building Blocks

This activity enhances critical-thinking, creative-thinking, and language skills.

Personal Time Capsule

The past comes alive when you open these memory capsules!

What You'll Need:

family photos and mementos

dated items, such as newspapers and magazines

child's art project

school worksheets

Spelling List
man
car
door
cat

paper

pen

durable container

Talk to the child about the concept of time capsules. Help her create one for herself or for the entire family. Make the first one a "one-week" capsule. Help the child collect suitable photos, mementos, publications, projects, and worksheets. In addition, ask the child to narrate her thoughts on various subjects and to list her favorite color, food, toy, friend, etc. Write down what she says and include it in the time capsule. Bury or hide it (if it is to be buried, make sure the container is airtight and waterproof). Then retrieve and open it at the appropriate time. Next, try a one-month capsule. After that, encourage the child to create one-year capsules, perhaps in connection with her birthday, major holidays, family vacations, or the end of the school year.

Building Blocks

This activity stimulates imagination and helps develop problem-solving skills.